HALLOWEEN UNMASKED

Discover the Secrets, Traditions, and Magic Behind the Ultimate Spooky Celebration

Lynda Corbett

Table of contents

CHAPTER 1: THE ORIGINS OF HALLOWEEN

1.1 The Ancient Roots of Samhain

Halloween, as we know it today, is a holiday rich in traditions and layered with centuries of evolution. Its origins date back more than 2,000 years to the ancient Celtic festival of Samhain (pronounced "sow-win"). Samhain, a Gaelic word meaning "summer's end," marked the conclusion of the harvest season and the beginning of the dark, cold winter months. For the Celts, who lived predominantly in what is now Ireland, the United Kingdom, and northern France, Samhain signified a time when the boundary between the living and the dead became blurred.

The Celts believed that on the night of October 31st, the veil between the physical world and the spirit world was thinnest. This allowed spirits, both benevolent and malevolent, to cross over into the world of the living. They viewed this as a critical time to appease the spirits of the dead and protect themselves from harmful forces.

In many ways, Samhain was a festival of transition—both in terms of the agricultural year and the supernatural realm. The Celts celebrated with bonfires, food, and offerings to honor their ancestors and placate wandering souls. Fires were central to the Samhain celebration. Communities would extinguish their hearth fires and relight them from a communal bonfire, symbolizing the renewal and protection of the home. It was also believed that the smoke from these fires could ward off evil spirits.

Another tradition during Samhain was the wearing of costumes, often made from animal skins. These disguises were meant to confuse or scare away spirits that might cause harm. Food and drink were offered to appease these entities, a practice that would eventually evolve into modern-day trick-or-treating.

Samhain was not merely a festival of fear and death, though. It was also a time to reflect on life, to celebrate the harvest that had just been gathered, and to prepare for the coming months of hardship. Druids, the Celtic priesthood, performed rituals and made predictions about the future, giving the people hope as they faced the uncertain months ahead. Samhain was a time for both reverence and celebration, a complex intersection of life and death, fear and festivity.

1.2 How Halloween Evolved Across Cultures

As Christianity began to spread across Europe, many of the pagan festivals, including Samhain, were incorporated into Christian traditions. In the 9th century, Pope Gregory IV declared November 1st as All Saints' Day, a day to honor all saints and martyrs of the Christian faith. The evening before, October 31st, became known as All Hallows' Eve, which later evolved into Halloween. This was a strategic move by the Church to Christianize pagan festivals, allowing people to maintain their customs but within a Christian framework.

Despite these changes, many of the original Celtic traditions persisted. In fact, they began to blend with the folklore and practices of other cultures as Halloween spread across Europe. For instance, in England, people would carve faces into turnips or beets and place candles inside them to ward off evil spirits—an early precursor to the modern jack-o'-lantern. This custom was rooted in the legend of Stingy Jack, a man who tricked the Devil and was doomed to wander the Earth with only a carved-out turnip to light his way.

In medieval Europe, Halloween also became a time for "souling," a tradition where the poor would go door to door offering prayers for the dead in exchange for food. This practice was particularly common on All Souls' Day, November 2nd, and can be seen as a direct ancestor to today's trick-or-treating. Children would visit homes in costume, reciting verses or prayers in exchange for "soul cakes," small pastries that symbolized the souls of the departed.

In Scotland and Ireland, the tradition of guising became popular. Children would dress in costume and go door to door, offering to perform songs, poems, or jokes in exchange for food or money. This custom of going house-to-house for offerings, combined with the belief that spirits roamed the earth, slowly developed into the Halloween we recognize today.

As Halloween spread to the United States in the 19th century, largely due to the influx of Irish and Scottish immigrants, the holiday began to take on a uniquely American flavor. By the early 20th century, Halloween had become a night of community events, with parties, parades, and festive gatherings. The emphasis shifted from honoring the dead to celebrating the living, particularly children.

1.3 From Superstition to Celebration: Halloween's Modern Transformation

The modern celebration of Halloween in the United States took shape in the early 20th century, with an increasing emphasis on fun, costumes, and community. However, the transformation of Halloween into the holiday we know today did not happen overnight—it was a gradual shift, influenced by changing societal values and commercial interests.

By the 1920s and 1930s, Halloween had evolved into a night of mischief, with young people engaging in pranks and practical jokes. This period saw a rise in vandalism and trickery, which led to efforts by civic and community organizations to redirect this youthful energy toward more organized activities like Halloween parties and parades. This was the beginning of the "trick-or-treat" culture that would dominate the mid-20th century.

The concept of trick-or-treating as we know it began to take hold in the 1930s and 1940s. It provided a way for children to participate in Halloween festivities in a more controlled and safe manner, offering them candy in exchange for refraining from mischief. This tradition exploded in popularity following World War II, when candy became more affordable, and suburban neighborhoods made trick-or-treating easier and safer for families.

As Halloween became more commercialized, candy companies, costume makers, and retailers saw an opportunity to capitalize on the holiday's growing appeal. By the 1950s, Halloween had become a major commercial event, with candy sales, costume contests, and haunted houses becoming integral parts of the celebration.

One of the most iconic symbols of modern Halloween is the jack-o'-lantern. While the tradition of carving faces into vegetables dates back to Celtic times, it wasn't until Irish immigrants brought the custom to America that pumpkins became the vegetable of choice. The availability and size of pumpkins made them perfect for carving, and by the late 19th century, they had become a staple of Halloween decorations.

Movies and media also played a significant role in shaping the modern Halloween experience. Horror films, particularly those centered around supernatural themes, began to dominate Halloween entertainment in the 20th century. Films like *Halloween* (1978) and *Nightmare on Elm Street* (1984) helped cement the connection between Halloween and the thrill of fear. These films, along with haunted houses and other attractions, transformed Halloween into a night of spooks and scares.

Despite its fun and festive nature, Halloween has not been without controversy. Some religious groups view the holiday as promoting paganism or occultism, while others criticize its commercialism. Yet, Halloween has endured as a cultural phenomenon, adapting to the times and reflecting society's evolving relationship with fear, community, and celebration.

In recent years, there has been a renewed interest in the more spiritual and cultural aspects of Halloween. Many people are once again exploring the holiday's roots in Samhain and other ancient traditions, seeking to reconnect with the deeper meaning of the holiday. This has led to a resurgence in interest in honoring ancestors, practicing mindfulness, and celebrating the cycles of nature.

Today, Halloween is one of the most celebrated holidays in the United States, with people of all ages participating in the festivities. From costume parties to haunted houses, trick-or-treating to pumpkin carving, Halloween has evolved into a multifaceted celebration that combines elements of its ancient past with the excitement and creativity of modern culture.

The origins of Halloween are deeply rooted in ancient customs and beliefs, yet the holiday has continually adapted and transformed to meet the needs and desires of the people who celebrate it. What began as a solemn festival honoring the dead has become a vibrant and joyous occasion, filled with creativity, community, and a little bit of spooky fun. As Halloween continues to evolve, it remains a reflection of our shared history and an opportunity to explore the mystery, magic, and wonder of the unknown.

CHAPTER 2: DIY HALLOWEEN: CRAFTS, COSTUMES, AND DECORATIONS

2.1 Eco-Friendly and Budget-Friendly Halloween

In today's world, sustainability has become a priority for many families. This trend extends to Halloween celebrations, where people are seeking ways to reduce waste, save money, and be more eco-conscious without sacrificing the festive spirit. Embracing an eco-friendly and budget-friendly Halloween doesn't mean sacrificing creativity or fun. In fact, it can lead to some of the most memorable and inventive celebrations.

One of the best ways to have an eco-friendly Halloween is by repurposing materials you already have around the house. Old clothes, cardboard boxes, fabric scraps, and household items can all be transformed into Halloween decorations, costumes, and party supplies with a little bit of creativity. This not only saves money but also reduces the need to buy new, mass-produced items that contribute to waste.

Costumes are often the first place to start when planning an eco-conscious Halloween. Instead of buying a new costume that may only be worn once, consider upcycling old clothes or thrift store finds. A worn-out dress can become the perfect base for a witch's costume, while an old sheet can be turned into a ghost outfit with a few strategic cuts. For more elaborate looks, accessories like hats, belts, and jewelry can often be sourced from thrift stores or made from things you already own.

If you're feeling crafty, try making costumes out of **recycled materials**. For example, cardboard boxes can be transformed into robot armor, cars, or even animal costumes with some paint and imagination. Recycled paper can be used to create masks, hats, or accessories like wings or crowns. Not only does this reduce waste, but it also gives your costume a personal, unique touch that can't be found in a store-bought outfit.

For **decorations**, opting for natural, reusable, or biodegradable materials can make a big difference. Pumpkins are a classic Halloween decoration that are not only festive but also eco-friendly. After carving, the insides can be used for cooking or composting, and the pumpkins themselves can be composted after the holiday. Instead of buying plastic decorations, try using natural elements like leaves, twigs, and gourds to create an autumnal atmosphere.

Recycled paper can also be used to make decorations like paper chains, garlands, or silhouettes of bats, ghosts, and spiders. These can be easily recycled after the holiday or stored for use next year. Another idea is to repurpose jars and cans as candle holders or lanterns, adding a spooky glow to your home.

When it comes to treats, consider **eco-friendly alternatives** to traditional candy packaging. Many Halloween treats come in individual plastic wrappers, which contribute to waste. Instead, consider making homemade treats like cookies, popcorn balls, or chocolate-dipped fruits. If you're not keen on making treats yourself, opt for candies wrapped in recyclable materials or look for eco-friendly candy brands that use sustainable packaging.

Hosting an eco-friendly Halloween party can also be a fun and rewarding experience. Skip disposable plates, cups, and utensils in favor of reusable or compostable options. Encourage guests to bring their own cups or dishes, or invest in reusable Halloween-themed dinnerware that you can use year after year. For party favors, consider giving out small, meaningful gifts like seeds for planting, reusable tote bags, or homemade crafts instead of plastic trinkets.

An eco-friendly Halloween not only helps the environment but can also make the holiday more meaningful and enjoyable. By focusing on creativity, sustainability, and personal touches, you can create a Halloween celebration that is both budget-friendly and earth-conscious.

2.2 Easy Costumes for Every Age: From Kids to Pets

Costumes are at the heart of Halloween, and the thrill of dressing up is something that appeals to all ages—from toddlers to adults, and even pets. The good news is that creating costumes doesn't have to be a stressful or expensive task. With a little imagination, you can put together costumes that are fun, affordable, and easy to make, ensuring that everyone—yes, even your pets—can get in on the Halloween spirit.

Kids' Costumes

When it comes to kids, the key is to keep it simple, comfortable, and fun. Often, kids are excited about their costumes but can quickly grow tired of outfits that are too elaborate or uncomfortable. Here are a few easy, age-appropriate costume ideas for children:

- **Superhero Capes**: A superhero cape is one of the easiest costumes to create. Use a piece of fabric or even an old bedsheet, cut it to the appropriate size, and tie it around the child's neck with a simple Velcro fastener. Add a mask or eye covering, and you've got a classic superhero outfit.
- **Animal Costumes**: Transform your child into a lion, cat, or bunny with simple costume elements. Use a headband to attach ears, a bit of face paint for whiskers, and a matching outfit in the appropriate color.
- **Fairy Wings**: For a whimsical fairy look, make wings from wire hangers bent into shape and covered with sheer fabric or pantyhose. Attach them to the back of a dress or jumpsuit, and finish the look with a wand made from a stick and ribbon.

Teen and Adult Costumes

For teens and adults, the focus is often on creativity and originality. Whether you're attending a Halloween party or just trick-or-treating with the kids, here are some easy, do-it-yourself costume ideas that require minimal effort but deliver maximum impact:

- **Mummy**: Wrap yourself in strips of white cloth or gauze bandages for a simple yet classic mummy look. To add a spooky touch, dab the fabric with tea or coffee to give it an aged appearance.
- **Zombie**: Transform into a zombie with old clothes, torn and distressed to look like they've been through an apocalypse. Add face paint or makeup to create a pale, gory complexion, and you're all set for the zombie apocalypse.
- **Classic Witch or Wizard**: A black dress, a pointy hat, and a broomstick are all you need for a classic witch costume. For wizards, add a long cloak, a wand (easily made from a stick or dowel), and a beard if you're going for the Merlin look.

Pet Costumes

Let's not forget our furry friends—pets can be a part of the Halloween fun too! Pet costumes should prioritize comfort and safety, but that doesn't mean they can't be adorable. Here are some easy pet costume ideas:

- **Pumpkin Pup**: A simple orange shirt with a green collar can transform your dog into a pumpkin. Add a felt leaf or stem to the collar for an extra touch.

- **Super Pet**: Just like for kids, a superhero cape is a quick and easy option for pets. Tie a piece of fabric around your pet's neck (make sure it's not too tight), and they're ready to save the day!
- **Pet Ballerina**: For smaller pets, use a piece of tulle to create a tutu. Attach it around the waist with a soft band, and your pet is ready for the Halloween ballet.

Costumes don't have to be complex or expensive to be impressive. With a little creativity and a few basic supplies, you can create fun, easy costumes that will delight children, adults, and pets alike.

2.3 Spooky Home Decor: Step-by-Step Decoration Ideas

Halloween is the perfect time to transform your home into a spooky, haunted space. Whether you're looking to create a few simple decorations or go all out with a haunted house theme, there are plenty of ways to add eerie touches to your home without breaking the bank. Here are some step-by-step decoration ideas to help you get started.

DIY Jack-o'-Lanterns

Carving pumpkins is a classic Halloween activity, and jack-o'-lanterns are one of the most iconic Halloween decorations. To make your own, follow these steps:

1. Choose a pumpkin that is the right size and shape for your design. Clean the exterior with a damp cloth.
2. Cut a circular hole in the top of the pumpkin and remove the lid. Use a spoon to scoop out the seeds and pulp.
3. Draw your design on the pumpkin with a marker. You can opt for a classic face, a spooky ghost, or something more elaborate.
4. Carefully carve along the lines using a small knife or pumpkin carving tool.
5. Place a candle or battery-operated light inside the pumpkin to illuminate your design.

Hanging Ghosts

To create a ghostly atmosphere in your home or yard, try making hanging ghosts from simple materials. Here's how:

1. Take a white sheet or piece of fabric and drape it over a small ball (a foam ball or a crumpled piece of paper works).
2. Tie a piece of string around the base of the ball to form the head.

3. Draw a spooky face on the fabric with a marker.

4. Use fishing wire or thread to hang your ghosts from trees, doorways, or ceilings for a spooky, floating effect.

Creepy Candle Holders

Add a spooky glow to your home with these DIY creepy candle holders:

1. Start with an empty glass jar or a wine bottle.
2. Drip red wax down the sides of the jar or bottle to create the appearance of blood.
3. Place a candle inside the jar (for safety, use battery-operated candles) and enjoy the eerie light it casts.

Spider Webs and Bats

Decorating with spider webs and bats can instantly transform any space into a haunted house. Here's how to make your own:

1. Stretch cotton or cheesecloth across windows, furniture, and walls to create spider webs. Add plastic spiders to complete the look.
2. Cut bat shapes out of black construction paper or cardboard. Hang them from strings or attach them to walls and windows for a spooky surprise.

Haunted House Entrance

Create a dramatic entrance to your haunted house with these simple steps:

1. Frame your front door with black crepe paper or fabric to create a dark, mysterious entryway.
2. Add cobwebs, plastic spiders, and glowing eyes (cut from cardboard and painted with glow-in-the-dark paint) to add to the spooky atmosphere.
3. Play eerie music or sound effects to greet your guests as they arrive.

Potion Bottles and Spell Books

For a witch's lair or mad scientist's laboratory theme, decorate your home with potion bottles and spell books:

1. Collect empty glass bottles and jars of various shapes and sizes.
2. Fill them with colored water, dried herbs, glitter, or other creepy concoctions.
3. Create labels for your bottles with names like "Bat Wings," "Eye of Newt," and "Witch's Brew."
4. Stack old books and bind them with string or leather to create spell books. Add handwritten pages or printouts with spooky incantations.

Outdoor Cemetery

Transform your yard into a spooky cemetery with these graveyard decorations:

1. Use cardboard or foam board to create tombstones of different shapes and sizes.
2. Paint the tombstones with gray or black paint and add names, dates, and spooky epitaphs.
3. Arrange the tombstones in your yard, sticking them into the ground or propping them against trees or bushes.
4. Scatter dried leaves, twigs, and cobwebs around the tombstones for an authentic graveyard feel.

Glowing Eyes in the Bushes

Create an eerie effect by adding glowing eyes to your bushes or trees:

1. Cut eye shapes out of cardboard or foam board.
2. Paint the eyes with glow-in-the-dark paint or attach glow sticks behind them.
3. Hide the eyes in bushes or trees around your yard for an unexpected scare.

Window Silhouettes

Use black construction paper or cardboard to create spooky silhouettes for your windows:

1. Draw or trace designs like witches, ghosts, bats, or skeletons onto black paper.
2. Cut out the shapes and tape them to the inside of your windows.
3. Illuminate the silhouettes with indoor lights or candles for a shadowy effect.

Decorating your home for Halloween is all about creating a spooky atmosphere that delights and surprises. Whether you prefer classic jack-o'-lanterns and hanging ghosts or more elaborate haunted house themes, DIY decorations allow you to customize your space and make Halloween truly memorable.

2.4 Planning the Perfect Halloween Party: Themes, Games, and More

Planning a Halloween party is an exciting opportunity to unleash your creativity and create a memorable event for friends, family, and neighbors. Whether you're hosting a small gathering or a larger bash, a well-planned Halloween party can be filled with spooky decorations, fun games, delicious treats, and themed activities that everyone will enjoy. Here's how to plan the perfect Halloween party, complete with themes, games, and more.

Choosing a Theme

One of the first decisions to make when planning your Halloween party is the theme. A theme can tie your decorations, costumes, games, and even food together, creating a cohesive and immersive experience for your guests. Here are some popular Halloween party themes to consider:

- **Haunted House**: Transform your home into a spooky haunted house with cobwebs, tombstones, and eerie lighting. Encourage guests to come in costume as ghosts, witches, or zombies.
- **Classic Monsters**: Celebrate iconic monsters like vampires, werewolves, and Frankenstein's monster with themed decorations and costumes. Serve "monster mash" cocktails and spooky finger foods.
- **Gothic Masquerade**: Host an elegant masquerade ball with a gothic twist. Decorate with black and red velvet, candelabras, and masks. Encourage guests to wear elaborate costumes and masks.
- **Pumpkin Patch Party**: Embrace the harvest season with a pumpkin-themed party. Decorate with pumpkins, gourds, and fall foliage. Serve pumpkin-flavored treats and host a pumpkin carving contest.

- **Witches and Wizards**: Invite guests to embrace their inner witch or wizard with a magical-themed party. Decorate with cauldrons, spell books, and mystical potions. Encourage guests to dress as their favorite magical characters.

Once you've chosen a theme, use it as inspiration for your party invitations, decorations, and activities to create a cohesive and immersive experience for your guests.

Decorating for Atmosphere

Create a spooky atmosphere for your Halloween party with themed decorations that reflect your chosen theme. Here are some ideas to get you started:

- **Creepy Lighting**: Use candles, string lights, and lanterns to create a dim, eerie ambiance throughout your home or outdoor space.
- **Haunted House Props**: Set up fake cobwebs, tombstones, and skeletons to create a haunted house vibe. Add spooky sound effects or music to enhance the atmosphere.
- **Themed Centerpieces**: Create themed centerpieces for tables using pumpkins, candles, and seasonal foliage. Incorporate elements like skulls, bats, or witch hats to tie into your theme.

- **Photo Booth**: Set up a photo booth area with props and backdrops that match your theme. Encourage guests to take photos in their costumes for lasting memories.

Decorations play a crucial role in setting the mood for your Halloween party, so take your time to plan and create a spooky atmosphere that will impress your guests.

Planning Halloween Games and Activities

Keep your guests entertained with Halloween-themed games and activities that everyone can enjoy. Here are some ideas for games and activities that are sure to be a hit:

- **Costume Contest**: Host a costume contest with categories like "Most Creative," "Scariest," and "Best Group Costume." Have guests vote for their favorites, and award prizes like gift cards or Halloween-themed trophies.
- **Pumpkin Carving Contest**: Provide pumpkins, carving tools, and stencils for guests to create their own jack-o'-lantern masterpieces. Award prizes for the spookiest, funniest, or most creative designs.
- **Haunted House Tour**: If your home is decorated like a haunted house, offer guided tours for guests to explore. Use spooky props, lighting

effects, and surprise scares to create a memorable experience.

- **Ghostly Treasure Hunt**: Hide small Halloween-themed treats or trinkets around your home or yard for guests to find. Provide clues or a treasure map to guide them on their ghostly adventure.
- **Mummy Wrap Relay**: Divide guests into teams and give each team a roll of toilet paper. One person from each team volunteers to be the mummy, and the others race to wrap them from head to toe. The first team to finish wins.

Games and activities are a great way to break the ice, get everyone involved, and keep the energy high throughout your Halloween party. Choose games that match your theme and appeal to guests of all ages for a memorable celebration.

Delicious Halloween Treats

No Halloween party is complete without delicious treats to satisfy your guests' sweet (or spooky) tooth. Serve a mix of savory and sweet snacks that tie into your party theme, and don't forget to include some classic Halloween favorites:

- **Candy Buffet**: Set up a candy buffet with bowls of assorted Halloween candies like candy corn, chocolate bars, and gummy worms. Use themed containers or jars for a festive display.

- **Pumpkin-themed Treats**: Serve pumpkin-shaped cookies, pumpkin pie, or pumpkin-flavored cupcakes for a taste of the season.
- **Savory Finger Foods**: Offer a variety of savory finger foods like mini sandwiches, cheese platters, and veggie trays. Label them with spooky names to fit your theme (e.g., "Witch's Fingers" for breadsticks).
- **Signature Cocktails and Mocktails**: Create themed cocktails and mocktails for adult guests to enjoy. Serve "Witch's Brew" punch or "Vampire's Kiss" cocktails garnished with red sugar rims.

Consider dietary restrictions and preferences when planning your menu, and offer options for guests who may prefer healthier or allergy-friendly alternatives.

Creating a Spooky Playlist

Set the mood for your Halloween party with a carefully curated playlist of spooky music and sound effects. Include classic Halloween songs like "Thriller" by Michael Jackson, "Monster Mash" by Bobby Pickett, and "Ghostbusters" by Ray Parker Jr. You can also add eerie sound effects like creaky doors, howling winds, and haunting screams to enhance the atmosphere.

Safety and Comfort

Lastly, ensure that your Halloween party is safe and comfortable for all guests. Provide adequate lighting, clear pathways, and supervision for activities like pumpkin carving or haunted house tours. Consider the age range and preferences of your guests when planning games and activities, and be mindful of any allergies or dietary restrictions when planning your menu.

By following these tips and ideas, you can plan a Halloween party that is both memorable and enjoyable for everyone. From themed decorations and activities to delicious treats and spooky music, your party is sure to be a hit with guests of all ages.

Spider Webs and Bats: DIY Halloween Decor

Creating your own spider webs and bats for Halloween is a fun, affordable way to add a spooky vibe to your home. These simple yet effective decorations can transform any space, whether indoors or outdoors, into a haunted haven. Here's how you can craft and use them to enhance your Halloween decor.

DIY Spider Webs

Spider webs are classic Halloween decorations, symbolizing haunted spaces and dark corners. Here are a few methods to create realistic and eerie spider webs:

1. Using Cotton Balls or Batting

- **Materials Needed:**
    1. Cotton balls or craft batting
    2. Scissors
    3. Tape or adhesive hooks
- **Instructions:**
    1. Pull apart cotton balls or batting into thin, irregular strands. The goal is to create a stretched, wispy look resembling real cobwebs.
    2. Once you have a web-like texture, stretch it across walls, doorways, or over furniture.
    3. Use tape or adhesive hooks to secure the ends of the webs in place.
    4. For an added touch, place plastic spiders onto the webs to make them more realistic.

2. Yarn Spider Web

- **Materials Needed:**
    1. White or black yarn
    2. Scissors
    3. Tape or thumbtacks
- **Instructions:**
    1. Cut several long pieces of yarn to serve as the base of your web. Tape or tack them

to a wall or in a corner, crossing them over each other in the shape of a star.
   2. To create the circular strands, weave another piece of yarn in a spiral shape from the center outwards, attaching it to each base strand as you go.
   3. Secure all ends with tape or thumbtacks. You can also place small toy spiders on the yarn to complete the look.

3. Hot Glue Webs

- **Materials Needed:**
   1. Hot glue gun
   2. Parchment paper
   3. Scissors
   4. White or glow-in-the-dark paint (optional)
- **Instructions:**
   1. Lay a piece of parchment paper flat on a table.
   2. Use the hot glue gun to draw a spider web design onto the parchment. Start with several intersecting lines, then connect them with circular strands.
   3. Allow the glue to cool and dry completely.

4. Once dry, peel the web off the parchment paper and use it as a window cling or hang it in a corner.

5. For an extra spooky touch, paint the web with white or glow-in-the-dark paint.

DIY Bats

Bats are another iconic Halloween symbol that add an eerie element to your decor. Here's how to make your own bats to decorate your home.

1. Paper Bats

- **Materials Needed:**
    1. Black construction paper or cardstock
    2. Scissors
    3. Pencil or chalk
    4. Double-sided tape or string
- **Instructions:**
    1. Draw bat shapes on black construction paper using a pencil or chalk. You can find bat templates online, or freehand your own design.
    2. Cut out the bat shapes carefully.
    3. Fold the wings slightly to give them a 3D effect.

4. Attach the bats to walls, doors, or windows with double-sided tape, or string them together to create a hanging garland.

5. You can also scatter the bats along a hallway or staircase for a dramatic look.

2. Hanging Bats

- **Materials Needed:**
    1. Black felt or foam sheets
    2. Scissors
    3. String or fishing line
    4. Glue or tape
- **Instructions:**
    1. Cut bat shapes out of black felt or foam sheets.
    2. Attach a small piece of string or fishing line to the top of each bat using glue or tape.
    3. Hang the bats from the ceiling, doorways, or tree branches outside to create a spooky, flying effect.
    4. Vary the heights and sizes of the bats to create a dynamic, swarming look.

3. Glow-in-the-Dark Bats

- **Materials Needed:**

1. Black glow-in-the-dark paper or regular black paper with glow paint
2. Scissors
3. Double-sided tape or string

- **Instructions:**
  1. Cut bat shapes out of glow-in-the-dark paper, or paint regular black paper bats with glow-in-the-dark paint.
  2. Attach the bats to walls or windows with tape, or hang them from the ceiling using string.
  3. These bats will emit a faint glow when the lights are off, creating a chilling, ghostly effect.

CHAPTER 3: SPOOKY RECIPES AND THEMED TREATS

Halloween is a time of indulgence, fun, and creativity, and this extends to the food. From creepy finger foods to allergy-friendly treats, there's something for everyone at the Halloween table. Whether you're hosting a party or just want to enjoy some festive snacks at home, this chapter will guide you through spooky recipes that capture the spirit of Halloween while satisfying every guest's dietary needs. Let's dive into themed treats and healthy alternatives that ensure everyone has a wickedly good time.

3.1 Halloween Party Food: Creepy Finger Foods and Drinks

A successful Halloween gathering isn't complete without a variety of themed foods and drinks that capture the holiday's eerie essence. Below are recipes for finger foods and drinks that look frightful but taste delicious, providing a perfect combination of fun and flavor.

Mummy Hot Dogs

These classic Halloween treats are easy to make and a hit with both kids and adults.

- **Ingredients:**
    1. Hot dogs (any type)
    2. Refrigerated crescent roll dough
    3. Mustard or ketchup for eyes
- **Instructions:**
    1. Preheat the oven to 375°F (190°C).
    2. Roll out the crescent dough and cut it into thin strips.
    3. Wrap each hot dog in the dough strips, leaving a gap for the "face."
    4. Bake for 12-15 minutes or until golden brown.
    5. Add small dots of mustard or ketchup for eyes.

Pumpkin Deviled Eggs

Give a classic appetizer a spooky twist by turning deviled eggs into little pumpkins.

- **Ingredients:**
    1. Hard-boiled eggs
    2. Mayonnaise
    3. Dijon mustard
    4. Paprika
    5. Green onion for stems
- **Instructions:**
    1. Halve the hard-boiled eggs and remove the yolks.
    2. Mix the yolks with mayonnaise, Dijon mustard, and a pinch of paprika.
    3. Spoon the yolk mixture back into the egg whites.
    4. Use a toothpick to create lines on the yolk, mimicking a pumpkin's ridges.
    5. Add a small piece of green onion to the top as a stem.

Witch's Broomstick Snacks

These savory broomsticks are a fun and easy snack for guests to nibble on.

- **Ingredients:**

1. Pretzel sticks
2. String cheese
3. Fresh chives

- **Instructions:**
    1. Cut the string cheese into thirds.
    2. Carefully slice the bottom half of each string cheese piece to create the bristles of the broom.
    3. Insert a pretzel stick into the top of the cheese.
    4. Use a chive to tie around the top of the cheese to complete the broom.

Blood Punch with Eyeballs

Serve your guests a chilling drink that's equal parts spooky and refreshing.

- **Ingredients:**
    1. Cranberry juice
    2. Lemon-lime soda
    3. Lychees (canned)
    4. Blueberries
- **Instructions:**
    1. Mix the cranberry juice and soda in a punch bowl.
    2. For the eyeballs, stuff a blueberry into the hollow center of each lychee.

3. Add the eyeball-stuffed lychees to the punch for a creepy floating effect.

Monster Nachos

These customizable nachos allow you to get creative with your toppings, creating faces and monsters on each plate.

- **Ingredients:**
    1. Tortilla chips
    2. Shredded cheese
    3. Salsa
    4. Sour cream
    5. Sliced olives, jalapeños, and tomatoes for decorations
- **Instructions:**
    1. Arrange the tortilla chips on a baking sheet and sprinkle with shredded cheese.
    2. Bake at 350°F (175°C) until the cheese is melted.
    3. Use sliced olives and jalapeños to create monster faces on each pile of nachos.
    4. Add dollops of sour cream to complete the look.

3.2 Vegan, Gluten-Free, and Allergy-Friendly Halloween Recipes

When planning a Halloween party or preparing treats, it's important to accommodate dietary restrictions to ensure everyone can enjoy the celebration. Below are a variety of vegan, gluten-free, and allergy-friendly recipes that are just as spooky and delicious as their traditional counterparts.

Vegan Ghost Cupcakes

These dairy-free cupcakes are adorable and spooky, perfect for vegans and non-vegans alike.

- **Ingredients:**
    1. 1 ½ cups all-purpose flour (or gluten-free flour)
    2. 1 cup sugar
    3. 1 tsp baking soda
    4. 1 tsp apple cider vinegar
    5. ½ cup vegetable oil
    6. 1 cup water
    7. Vanilla frosting (dairy-free)
    8. Mini chocolate chips for eyes
- **Instructions:**
    1. Preheat the oven to 350°F (175°C) and line a cupcake tin with liners.

2. In a large bowl, mix the flour, sugar, and baking soda.
3. Add the oil, water, and apple cider vinegar, stirring until smooth.
4. Pour the batter into the cupcake liners and bake for 20-25 minutes.
5. Once cooled, frost the cupcakes with the dairy-free vanilla frosting, creating ghost shapes.
6. Add mini chocolate chips for the eyes.

Gluten-Free "Witch Fingers"

These gluten-free, almond-flavored cookies are shaped like witch fingers, complete with almond "nails."

- **Ingredients:**
    1. 1 cup almond flour
    2. ¼ cup coconut flour
    3. ½ cup sugar
    4. 1 tsp vanilla extract
    5. ½ cup vegan butter
    6. Almond slices for nails
    7. Red food coloring for blood (optional)
- **Instructions:**
    1. Preheat the oven to 350°F (175°C).
    2. In a bowl, mix the almond flour, coconut flour, sugar, vanilla, and vegan butter until a dough forms.

3. Roll the dough into finger-like shapes.

4. Press an almond slice onto the end of each cookie to form a "nail."

5. If desired, add red food coloring around the base of the almond for a bloody effect.

6. Bake for 10-12 minutes until golden brown.

Nut-Free Spooky Popcorn Balls

These allergy-friendly popcorn balls are safe for kids with nut allergies and can be shaped into fun Halloween characters.

- **Ingredients:**
    1. 10 cups popped popcorn
    2. 3 tbsp vegan butter
    3. 4 cups marshmallows
    4. Orange food coloring
    5. Candy eyeballs or mini chocolate chips
- **Instructions:**
    1. Melt the vegan butter and marshmallows in a large pot over medium heat.
    2. Stir in the food coloring until the mixture turns a spooky orange color.
    3. Pour the mixture over the popcorn and stir until coated.
    4. Let the popcorn cool slightly, then shape it into balls.

5. Add candy eyeballs or mini chocolate chips to create spooky faces.

Vegan "Pumpkin" Soup

This hearty, warming soup is perfect for a Halloween dinner, with no animal products involved.

- **Ingredients:**
    1. 1 small pumpkin (or canned pumpkin puree)
    2. 1 can coconut milk
    3. 1 onion, chopped
    4. 2 cloves garlic, minced
    5. Vegetable broth
    6. Spices: cinnamon, nutmeg, salt, and pepper
- **Instructions:**
    1. If using fresh pumpkin, roast it in the oven until tender. Once roasted, scoop out the flesh.
    2. In a large pot, sauté the onions and garlic until softened.
    3. Add the pumpkin, coconut milk, and vegetable broth, stirring until well combined.
    4. Season with cinnamon, nutmeg, salt, and pepper to taste.

5. Simmer for 20 minutes, then blend until smooth. Serve hot.

3.3 Healthy Halloween Treats for Kids and Families

Halloween doesn't have to be all about sugary treats. It's possible to offer healthier alternatives that are still fun and festive. Here are a few creative ideas for making Halloween-themed snacks that kids and families will love without the sugar rush.

Apple Monsters

These adorable apple slices are transformed into monsters with the help of peanut butter, fruit, and a little imagination.

- **Ingredients:**
    1. Apples, sliced
    2. Peanut butter (or sunflower seed butter for nut allergies)
    3. Strawberries, sliced
    4. Mini marshmallows or raisins
- **Instructions:**
    1. Spread peanut butter on one side of the apple slice.

2. Use the strawberry slice as a tongue, placing it between two apple slices.
3. Stick mini marshmallows or raisins on top as eyes.

Banana Ghosts and Orange Pumpkins

A simple and healthy way to make fruit more festive.

- **Ingredients:**
    1. Bananas
    2. Mini chocolate chips
    3. Oranges
    4. Celery sticks
- **Instructions:**
    1. Peel and halve the bananas. Stick mini chocolate chips into the bananas to create ghost faces.
    2. Peel the oranges and insert a small piece of celery into the top to resemble pumpkin stems.

Jack-O'-Lantern Stuffed Peppers

These stuffed peppers are both festive and nutritious, with a Halloween twist.

- **Ingredients:**
    1. 4 orange bell peppers
    2. 1 cup quinoa

3. 1 can black beans, drained
4. 1 cup corn
5. Salsa
6. Shredded cheese (optional)

- **Instructions:**
   1. Cook the quinoa according to package instructions.
   2. Mix the quinoa, black beans, corn, and salsa together in a bowl.
   3. Cut the tops off the bell peppers and scoop out the seeds.
   4. Carefully carve jack-o'-lantern faces into each pepper.
   5. Fill the peppers with the quinoa mixture.
   6. Bake at 350°F (175°C) for 20-25 minutes. Add cheese on top if desired.

By offering a mix of traditional, allergy-friendly, and healthy treats, you can ensure that everyone at your Halloween celebration has a fun and tasty experience. These spooky and themed recipes are sure to impress your guests, whether they're looking for creepy finger foods, vegan alternatives, or nutritious snacks. With a little creativity and some ghoulish inspiration, your Halloween feast will be one to remember.

CHAPTER 4: GHOST STORIES AND SPOOKY LEGENDS

Halloween has long been associated with the supernatural, offering a time when the veil between the living and the dead is believed to be at its thinnest. In this chapter, we will dive into the chilling world of haunted tales, ghostly apparitions, and eerie urban legends that have both terrified and fascinated people for centuries. From ancient myths to real-life haunting experiences

4.1 Haunted Tales: Halloween's Scariest Myths and Legends

Halloween's origins in the ancient Celtic festival of Samhain, when it was believed spirits roamed the earth, have given rise to a variety of myths and legends. Some of these tales are rooted in ancient lore, while others have evolved into modern-day ghost stories that continue to send shivers down our spines.

The Legend of the Headless Horseman

One of Halloween's most famous legends comes from Washington Irving's *The Legend of Sleepy Hollow*, which tells the story of a ghostly figure known as the Headless Horseman. This specter, believed to be the ghost of a Hessian soldier from the Revolutionary War, is said to haunt the town of Sleepy Hollow, New York, in search of his lost head.

According to the legend, the Headless Horseman rides through the night, terrorizing locals as he hunts for a replacement head. The story's protagonist, Ichabod Crane, is chased by the Horseman, only to disappear mysteriously, leaving behind his shattered pumpkin—leading many to believe that the Headless Horseman claimed him as a victim. This chilling tale has become an enduring symbol of Halloween, epitomizing the fear of the unknown and the idea of restless spirits seeking vengeance.

The Banshee: A Wailing Harbinger of Death

In Irish mythology, the Banshee is a ghostly figure whose presence signals an impending death. This female spirit is often described as a pale, spectral woman with long, flowing hair and a mournful, bone-chilling wail that echoes through the night. Her appearances are said to foretell the death of a loved one, striking fear into the hearts of those who hear her cries.

The Banshee's origins date back to ancient Ireland, where she was considered a spirit linked to particular families, often appearing to warn them of tragedy. While her appearance varies from legend to legend—sometimes she is beautiful, other times grotesque—her role remains the same: to announce death and mourn for the souls about to depart from this world.

The Bloody Mary Legend

One of the most famous urban legends associated with Halloween and the supernatural is the tale of Bloody Mary. According to the legend, if you stand in front of a mirror in a darkened room, light a candle, and chant "Bloody Mary" three times, the ghost of a vengeful woman will appear in the reflection, ready to drag you into the mirror world or scratch your face with her claws.

The origins of the Bloody Mary legend are shrouded in mystery, but some believe it is based on historical figures such as Mary I of England, also known as "Bloody Mary" for her persecution of Protestants. Others think it might be linked to the folklore of a witch or ghost seeking revenge. Regardless of its origins, the legend of Bloody Mary continues to frighten people who dare to try summoning her, especially on Halloween night.

The Black-Eyed Children

A more modern legend, but one that has gained widespread notoriety, is the unsettling tale of the Black-Eyed Children. These ghostly children are said to appear at night, knocking on doors and asking for help. What makes them terrifying is their pitch-black eyes and their insistence that they be let inside.

According to witnesses, these children evoke an overwhelming sense of dread and unease. Once their eyes are revealed, the person who encounters them often experiences intense fear and quickly shuts the door. Though there is no definitive explanation for the Black-Eyed Children, they have been linked to everything from aliens and demons to lost souls trying to find their way back to the living world.

4.2 Ghosts, Ghouls, and Eerie Urban Legends

Beyond traditional myths, Halloween also brings to mind eerie urban legends and ghostly apparitions that have been passed down through generations. These stories often blur the line between fact and fiction, leaving listeners wondering if they could actually be true.

La Llorona: The Weeping Woman

One of the most haunting legends from Latin American folklore is the story of *La Llorona*, or "The Weeping Woman." According to legend, La Llorona was once a beautiful woman named Maria who drowned her children in a fit of rage or despair after being abandoned by her lover. Overcome with guilt, she drowned herself as well, but her spirit was condemned to wander the earth in search of her lost children.

La Llorona is often described as a ghostly figure in a white dress, weeping and calling out for her children near rivers and bodies of water. Her cries of "¡Ay, mis hijos!" ("Oh, my children!") are said to strike fear into the hearts of those who hear them, as encountering La Llorona is believed to bring misfortune or even death.

The Vanishing Hitchhiker

The Vanishing Hitchhiker is one of the most well-known urban legends and has been told in various forms across different cultures. The story typically involves a driver who picks up a hitchhiker late at night. After a short conversation, the hitchhiker asks to be dropped off at a specific location, often near a cemetery. When the driver turns to speak to the passenger again, they find that the hitchhiker has vanished without a trace.

The driver later learns that the hitchhiker was a ghost, often a young woman who died tragically near the location where they were picked up. The Vanishing Hitchhiker tale plays on themes of loss, longing, and the eerie possibility that the dead are still among us, seeking a final destination they'll never reach.

The Hookman

This classic urban legend is a staple of ghost stories told around campfires or at Halloween parties. The story goes that a young couple is parked at a secluded spot when they hear a report on the radio about an escaped murderer with a hook for a hand. Terrified, the couple decides to leave, only to later discover a bloody hook hanging from the car door handle.

The Hookman legend taps into the fear of being vulnerable in isolated places, as well as the idea that danger can strike at any moment, even during what should be a peaceful or romantic night out. It's a tale that has stood the test of time, continuing to be retold as a cautionary story about the perils of letting your guard down.

Slender Man

A more recent urban legend that gained notoriety on the internet is Slender Man, a tall, faceless figure who is said to stalk and abduct children. Slender Man is often depicted as wearing a black suit and having unnaturally long arms, which he uses to lure or ensnare his victims. Though Slender Man started as a fictional character created for an online horror contest, he quickly became an iconic figure in modern folklore, with many believing that the stories about him are based on real sightings.

Slender Man's rise to fame demonstrates the power of the internet in spreading urban legends and the way these stories evolve to reflect modern fears. Despite being a relatively new addition to the world of spooky legends, Slender Man has become one of the most enduring and terrifying figures in contemporary horror.

4.3 Reader Submissions: Real-Life Haunting Experiences

While myths and urban legends are fascinating, there's nothing quite as chilling as real-life haunting experiences shared by those who've lived through them. Below are a few submissions from readers who have encountered the supernatural in their own lives, making these tales all the more frightening.

The Haunted Hotel Room

"I was staying at an old hotel while traveling for work, and I was the only guest on my floor. That night, I woke up to the sound of heavy footsteps pacing outside my door. At first, I thought it was a staff member, but the footsteps never stopped—they just kept pacing back and forth. I got up to check the hallway, but when I opened the door, no one was there. The footsteps continued for another hour, growing louder and more frantic. I barely slept that night, and I later found out that the hotel was rumored to be haunted by a former guest who never checked out."

The Shadow in the Mirror

"When I was a kid, I used to see a shadowy figure standing in the corner of my bedroom at night. It didn't have any distinguishable features, but I could feel it watching me. One night, I was brushing my teeth in the bathroom and caught a glimpse of the same shadow in the mirror, standing behind me. I spun around, but nothing was there. After that, the figure stopped appearing, but I still get chills every time I look in a mirror at night."

The Ghostly Roommate

"I moved into a new apartment and started noticing strange things happening. My keys would disappear and reappear in places I hadn't left them, and I would hear faint voices when no one else was around. One night, I woke up to the sound of someone whispering my name. I sat up and saw a faint figure standing at the foot of my bed. It was a woman in old-fashioned clothing, just staring at me. I blinked, and she was gone. After that, I started referring to her as my 'ghost roommate,' and while she never appeared again, I couldn't shake the feeling that I wasn't alone in that apartment."

CHAPTER 5: THE DARK PSYCHOLOGY OF FEAR

Fear is one of the most powerful emotions we experience. It can cause us to jump, scream, or even freeze in terror. But what's fascinating about fear is that many of us actively seek it out, especially during Halloween. We attend haunted houses, watch horror movies, and share scary stories, all in the name of fun.

5.1 Why We Love Being Scared: The Psychology Behind Halloween Thrills

Fear may seem like an emotion we'd want to avoid, yet we often pursue activities that are designed to frighten us. From Halloween haunted houses to horror movie marathons, we willingly immerse ourselves in scary environments. Why do we do this, and what's the appeal of being scared?

The Thrill Factor: The Adrenaline Rush

One of the main reasons people enjoy being scared is the adrenaline rush that comes with it. Fear triggers the body's fight-or-flight response, releasing a surge of adrenaline and other chemicals like dopamine, which heighten our senses and create a natural "high." This physiological response can feel exhilarating, especially when we know deep down that we are safe. The key is that we are engaging with fear in a controlled environment, such as a haunted house or a horror film, where we can experience the thrill of fear without real danger.

This controlled exposure to fear allows us to push our boundaries and explore emotions we might otherwise avoid in daily life. The sense of relief we feel after surviving a scare also provides a cathartic release, creating a cycle where the fear builds up, climaxes, and then dissipates, leaving us with a sense of accomplishment or even euphoria.

The Brain's Love for Novelty and Uncertainty

The human brain is wired to seek novelty and stimulation, and fear can provide both. Scary situations often introduce unexpected elements—sudden movements, eerie sounds, or disturbing imagery—which activate parts of the brain responsible for alertness and attention. This keeps us on edge, constantly anticipating what might happen next.

Fear also taps into our love for uncertainty. When we watch a horror movie or enter a haunted house, we know we're going to be scared, but we don't know exactly how or when. This uncertainty creates suspense, which is key to making fear enjoyable. It engages our brain's reward system, leading us to crave the resolution of that suspense, which comes in the form of a jump scare or plot twist. This element of surprise is crucial in maintaining our interest and excitement throughout the experience.

Social Bonding and Shared Experiences

Fear can also bring people closer together. Watching a horror movie with friends or walking through a haunted house as a group creates a shared experience that can strengthen social bonds. When we're scared, we tend to seek comfort from others, whether it's grabbing a friend's arm during a scary scene or laughing together after a particularly intense moment.

This social aspect of fear is deeply ingrained in human nature. Historically, humans relied on social groups for survival, and experiencing fear together would have reinforced group cohesion and mutual support. Today, these same dynamics play out when we engage in fear-based activities with others, making the experience not only more enjoyable but also more memorable.

A Safe Way to Confront Real-World Fears

Engaging with fictional or controlled fear can also serve as a way to process real-world anxieties. Watching a horror movie or telling ghost stories allows us to confront fears of death, danger, or the unknown in a safe and symbolic way. The monsters, ghosts, and villains in these stories often represent deeper, subconscious fears that we carry with us.

By facing these fears in a controlled setting, we can gain a sense of mastery over them. It's a way to confront the things that scare us without putting ourselves in actual harm's way. This can be especially therapeutic for people dealing with anxiety or phobias, as it allows them to engage with fear on their own terms and in a way that they can manage.

5.2 Horror Films and Haunted Houses: How Fear is Designed

Fear, when used as a form of entertainment, isn't random—it's carefully crafted to maximize the emotional response from the audience. Whether it's a horror film, a haunted house, or a spooky attraction, fear is designed through a combination of psychological principles, sensory manipulation, and storytelling techniques.

The Role of Suspense and Tension in Horror Films

Horror films are masters at building suspense and tension, using pacing, sound, and visual cues to create a sense of dread. Directors often rely on the "slow burn" approach, gradually escalating the tension throughout the movie to keep the audience on edge. This buildup is crucial because it taps into our natural fear of the unknown. The longer we wait for something to happen, the more anxious we become, which makes the eventual scare all the more effective.

Another common technique is the use of music and sound effects. Eerie soundscapes, unsettling noises, and sudden loud bangs are all designed to heighten the emotional impact of a scene. Silence is also used effectively in horror, as it creates a vacuum that the audience knows will soon be filled with something terrifying. This manipulation of sound and silence keeps viewers in a heightened state of awareness, ready to jump at the next scare.

The Psychology of Jump Scares

Jump scares are one of the most effective tools in horror, taking advantage of our startle reflex. This reflex is an automatic response to sudden stimuli, such as loud noises or unexpected movements, and is deeply ingrained in our biology as a survival mechanism. In a horror film or haunted house, jump scares exploit this reflex to create an immediate, intense reaction.

But jump scares are only effective when used sparingly and with proper buildup. If they're overused, the audience becomes desensitized, and the scares lose their impact. Skilled horror filmmakers know how to balance suspense with shock, using misdirection to keep the audience guessing and ensuring that each scare lands with maximum effect.

Haunted Houses: Immersive Fear Experiences

Haunted houses take fear to the next level by immersing participants in a physical environment designed to evoke terror. These attractions often combine visual effects, actors, sound, and tactile elements to create a multi-sensory experience that overwhelms the senses.

The key to a successful haunted house is its ability to create a sense of vulnerability. Participants know they're in a safe environment, but the combination of disorienting visuals, unexpected scares, and the presence of actors who can physically interact with them makes it feel real in the moment. This immersion allows participants to experience fear on a visceral level, activating their fight-or-flight response in a way that few other forms of entertainment can achieve.

5.3 Folklore and Fear: The Role of Scary Stories in Culture

Fear has been a central theme in folklore and storytelling for centuries. Scary stories serve a variety of purposes in culture, from imparting moral lessons to explaining natural phenomena and reinforcing social norms. They also provide a way for people to confront their deepest fears in a safe, symbolic manner.

The Power of Folklore in Shaping Beliefs and Behaviors

Throughout history, many cultures have used fear-based stories as a way to influence behavior. In some cases, these stories were meant to teach lessons or warn against dangerous actions. For example, in many European folktales, the figure of the witch was used to represent the dangers of straying from societal norms or venturing into the unknown. By casting certain behaviors or places as "dangerous," these stories helped to reinforce cultural values and maintain social order.

In other cases, scary stories were used to explain natural phenomena that people couldn't otherwise understand. For instance, before the advent of modern science, stories of ghosts or spirits were often used to explain sudden deaths, diseases, or natural disasters. These stories provided a way to make sense of a chaotic world and gave people a sense of control over forces that seemed beyond their understanding.

Ghost Stories: Cultural Reflections of Fear

Ghost stories are a universal form of folklore, with nearly every culture having its own version of spirits that haunt the living. These stories often reflect the cultural values and fears of the time. In many Asian cultures, for example, ghosts are seen as restless spirits who are unable to move on because of unresolved issues, such as unfulfilled obligations or improper burial rites. These stories emphasize the importance of family, honor, and tradition, and serve as a reminder of the consequences of neglecting these duties.

In Western cultures, ghost stories often focus on themes of guilt, revenge, and unfinished business. The ghosts in these stories are frequently seeking justice or retribution for wrongs committed against them in life, serving as a warning to those who mistreat others. These tales tap into deep-seated fears about morality, death, and the possibility of life after death.

Urban Legends: Modern Scary Stories

Urban legends are the modern-day equivalent of folklore, often reflecting contemporary fears and anxieties. Stories of haunted houses, cursed objects, or mysterious creatures like Bigfoot or the Loch Ness Monster tap into our collective fear of the unknown. These stories are often spread through word of mouth or the internet, evolving as they're retold, much like traditional folktales.

One of the reasons urban legends are so effective is that they're often framed as being based on real events, blurring the line between fiction and reality. This makes them all the more terrifying because they feel plausible. Even in our modern, technology-driven world, we're still drawn to stories that challenge our sense of safety and security.

The Role of Fear in Cultural Rituals

Fear also plays a role in many cultural rituals, particularly those associated with death and the afterlife. In Mexico, for example, the Day of the Dead is a celebration that honors deceased loved ones while also confronting the fear of death. The rituals surrounding this holiday, such as building altars and offering food to the dead, are designed to show respect for the dead while also acknowledging the inevitability of death.

Similarly, Halloween in Western cultures is a time when people confront their fears of death, darkness, and the supernatural. The tradition of dressing up in costumes, carving pumpkins, and telling ghost stories can be traced back to ancient festivals like Samhain, where people would ward off evil spirits by disguising themselves. These rituals allow people to engage with fear in a playful and symbolic way, making it more manageable.

Fear is a complex and multifaceted emotion that has fascinated humans for centuries. Whether it's the adrenaline rush of a haunted house, the suspense of a horror film, or the moral lessons of a ghost story, fear plays a central role in our entertainment, culture, and psychology. By understanding the dark psychology of fear, we can appreciate why we seek out scary experiences and how they help us confront and manage the fears that lurk in the shadows of our minds.

CHAPTER 6: HALLOWEEN AROUND THE WORLD

Halloween is celebrated in many countries, but each region adds its unique twist to the festivities. While the United States has popularized the spooky holiday with trick-or-treating, haunted houses, and costumes, other countries have their own ways of honoring the dead and embracing the eerie. From Japan's cultural reverence for spirits to Mexico's vibrant *Día de los Muertos* festival, this chapter explores how different parts of the world celebrate Halloween and similar traditions.

6.1 Global Halloween Traditions: From the U.S. to Japan

The way Halloween is celebrated in various countries around the world reflects a fascinating blend of local customs, historical beliefs, and modern influences. While many nations have adopted elements of American-style Halloween, such as dressing up in costumes and carving pumpkins, there are still distinct differences in how the holiday is observed.

Halloween in the United States: The Epicenter of the Holiday

The United States is widely regarded as the epicenter of modern Halloween celebrations. In America, Halloween is all about fun and fright, with people of all ages donning costumes, attending parties, and decorating their homes with spooky themes. One of the most iconic elements of Halloween in the U.S. is trick-or-treating, where children go door-to-door collecting candy from neighbors. This tradition, believed to have originated from European customs of "souling" and "guising," has evolved into a family-friendly activity that brings communities together.

In addition to trick-or-treating, haunted houses and Halloween-themed amusement parks are popular across the U.S., offering thrills and chills for those seeking more intense scares. Americans also participate in carving pumpkins into jack-o'-lanterns, hosting costume parties, and watching classic horror films. The commercialization of Halloween in the U.S. is significant, with millions of dollars spent annually on costumes, candy, and decorations.

Halloween in the United Kingdom: Echoes of Samhain

In the United Kingdom, Halloween has its roots in ancient Celtic traditions, particularly the festival of Samhain. Celebrated on October 31st, Samhain marked the end of the harvest season and the beginning of winter. It was believed that on this night, the boundary between the living and the dead was blurred, allowing spirits to cross over into the world of the living. To protect themselves, people would light bonfires and wear costumes to disguise themselves from wandering spirits.

Modern Halloween celebrations in the U.K. are similar to those in the U.S., with children dressing up in costumes and trick-or-treating. However, the holiday hasn't reached the same level of commercialization. In Scotland and Ireland, where the Celtic roots of Halloween are strongest, traditional games like *bobbing for apples* and telling ghost stories are still common.

Halloween in Japan: A New Cultural Phenomenon

Halloween in Japan is a relatively recent phenomenon, but it has rapidly gained popularity, especially in large cities like Tokyo. The holiday was introduced to Japan through American pop culture, but it has since been embraced in a uniquely Japanese way. Unlike in the U.S., where trick-or-treating is a central activity,

Halloween in Japan is more focused on costumes and public events.

One of the highlights of Halloween in Japan is the Shibuya Halloween Street Party, where thousands of people gather in elaborate costumes to celebrate in the heart of Tokyo. Cosplay, which is already popular in Japan, fits naturally into Halloween celebrations, with participants dressing as characters from anime, manga, movies, and video games. Parades and costume contests are common, and major theme parks like Tokyo Disneyland and Universal Studios Japan hold special Halloween-themed events.

Japan's approach to Halloween emphasizes creativity, community, and aesthetics, making it less about horror and more about having fun in costume. While spooky decorations and haunted attractions exist, they are not as central to the holiday as in Western countries.

Halloween in Mexico: A Prelude to Día de los Muertos

In Mexico, Halloween (or *Noche de Brujas*, meaning "Night of the Witches") is celebrated on October 31st, but it is often seen as a prelude to the much more significant holiday, *Día de los Muertos* (Day of the Dead), which takes place on November 1st and 2nd. Halloween in Mexico has taken on some elements of the

American version, with children dressing up in costumes and going trick-or-treating in some areas. However, the real focus of Mexican culture during this time is on honoring the dead through *Día de los Muertos*, a celebration of life, death, and remembrance.

While Halloween in Mexico may feature spooky costumes and parties, *Día de los Muertos* is a more vibrant and meaningful holiday, blending indigenous traditions with Catholic influences.

Halloween in Germany: *Gruselnacht*

In Germany, Halloween is known as *Gruselnacht*, or "Night of Horrors." Although the holiday is relatively new to the country, it has grown in popularity over the years, especially among younger generations. Germans now embrace many of the same traditions seen in the U.S., such as dressing up in costumes, throwing parties, and decorating homes with spooky themes.

One unique aspect of German Halloween celebrations is the emphasis on "scary" costumes. Unlike in the U.S., where people might dress as anything from superheroes to animals, German costumes tend to focus more on traditional Halloween themes like witches, zombies, and skeletons. Halloween in Germany is also influenced by local customs, such as the celebration of *Allerheiligen*

(All Saints' Day) on November 1st, which is a public holiday in some regions.

Halloween in Ireland: Returning to Its Celtic Roots

Ireland, the birthplace of Halloween's Celtic predecessor, Samhain, has embraced the holiday with gusto. Today, Halloween in Ireland is marked by festivals, bonfires, fireworks, and costume parties. Dublin's *Bram Stoker Festival*, named after the author of *Dracula*, is one of the most famous Halloween events in the country, celebrating all things spooky with theater, film screenings, and haunted tours.

Ireland's Halloween traditions also include some of the old Celtic customs, such as lighting bonfires and playing traditional games like *snap-apple* (similar to bobbing for apples). Trick-or-treating is common among children, and adults often participate in costume contests and ghost story gatherings.

6.2 Unique Festivals and Rituals That Celebrate the Dead

While Halloween is widely known for its spooky elements, many cultures around the world have their own unique festivals and rituals that celebrate the dead in a more reverent and meaningful way. These festivals often reflect deep cultural beliefs about the afterlife, death, and the connection between the living and the dead.

Obon Festival in Japan: Honoring Ancestors

The Obon Festival is one of Japan's most important holidays, dedicated to honoring deceased ancestors. Held in mid-August, Obon is a time when families come together to remember their loved ones and offer prayers for their spirits. The belief is that the spirits of ancestors return to the world of the living during Obon to visit their families, and various rituals are performed to guide them back to the afterlife.

One of the most iconic elements of the Obon Festival is the *Toro Nagashi*, or the floating of lanterns. During this ceremony, people place lanterns with candles on rivers, lakes, or the sea to light the way for the spirits' journey back to the spirit world. While not as spooky as Halloween, Obon shares a similar theme of connecting the living with the dead and acknowledging the spiritual presence of ancestors.

Pchum Ben in Cambodia: Feeding the Spirits

Pchum Ben is a 15-day Buddhist festival in Cambodia that honors deceased ancestors. It takes place in late

September or early October and is one of the most important religious events in the country. During Pchum Ben, Cambodians visit pagodas to offer food and other gifts to monks, who then pass these offerings on to the spirits of the dead.

The belief is that during Pchum Ben, the gates of the underworld open, and the spirits of the deceased return to the earth. Some of these spirits are believed to be suffering, and the offerings made by the living can help alleviate their suffering. The festival is a time for reflection, family gatherings, and prayers for the dead.

Chuseok in South Korea: A Harvest Festival and Ancestor Worship

Chuseok is a major harvest festival in South Korea, but it is also a time to honor deceased ancestors. Celebrated in September or October, Chuseok is often compared to Thanksgiving, as families come together to give thanks for the year's harvest. However, Chuseok also includes rituals known as *Charye*, where families prepare food and offer it to their ancestors at their gravesites.

This act of ancestor worship is an essential part of Chuseok, reflecting the deep respect that Koreans have for their forebears. By offering food and performing rituals, families ensure that their ancestors are cared for in the afterlife, while also strengthening the bond between the living and the dead.

Pitru Paksha in India: Paying Homage to Ancestors

Pitru Paksha is a Hindu festival in India dedicated to honoring ancestors and ensuring their peaceful passage to the afterlife. The festival lasts for 16 days, usually falling in September or October. During Pitru Paksha, families perform rituals and offer food to their ancestors, believing that these offerings will help them achieve liberation from the cycle of rebirth.

One of the key rituals of Pitru Paksha is *Shradh*, a ceremony in which families perform prayers and offer food, water, and other gifts to the spirits of their deceased relatives. The festival is a time for reflection, gratitude, and connecting with one's lineage.

Hungry Ghost Festival in China: Appeasing Restless Spirits

The Hungry Ghost Festival, celebrated in China and other parts of East Asia, is a time to honor and appease restless spirits who are believed to roam the earth during the seventh month of the lunar calendar. The festival is also known as the Ghost Month, and it is believed that during this time, the gates of the underworld are opened, allowing ghosts to enter the world of the living.

To avoid bad luck and misfortune, people offer food, incense, and other gifts to the spirits. Paper money and symbolic items are also burned to provide for the ghosts in the afterlife. The Hungry Ghost Festival is a time for reflection on mortality, as well as an opportunity to protect oneself from the malevolent influence of unhappy spirits.

6.3 Día de los Muertos: The Mexican Celebration of Life and Death

One of the most well-known and unique festivals celebrating the dead is Mexico's *Día de los Muertos* (Day of the Dead), which takes place on November 1st and 2nd. Unlike Halloween, which often focuses on fear and the supernatural, *Día de los Muertos* is a joyful and vibrant celebration of life, death, and the enduring bond between the living and the deceased. Rooted in indigenous Aztec traditions and blended with Catholic elements, *Día de los Muertos* is a time for families to honor their ancestors and celebrate their memories.

The Origins and Significance of *Día de los Muertos*

The origins of *Día de los Muertos* can be traced back to ancient Mesoamerican cultures, particularly the Aztecs, who believed that death was not the end of life but rather a transition to another realm. The festival originally lasted for an entire month and was dedicated to the goddess Mictecacihuatl, the "Lady of the Dead." After the Spanish colonization of Mexico, Catholic traditions were incorporated into the indigenous customs, and the festival was moved to coincide with All Saints' Day and All Souls' Day on November 1st and 2nd.

During *Día de los Muertos*, families build *ofrendas* (altars) in their homes or at gravesites to honor their deceased loved ones. These altars are decorated with photos, candles, marigold flowers, and the favorite foods and drinks of the departed. The belief is that the spirits of the dead return to the world of the living during this time, and the offerings on the altar help guide them on their journey.

Far from being a somber occasion, *Día de los Muertos* is a time of joy and celebration, as families come together to remember the lives of their loved ones and celebrate their enduring presence. The festival is filled with music, dancing, and colorful decorations, such as *calacas* (skeletons) and *calaveras* (sugar skulls), which symbolize the playful and cyclical nature of life and death.

The Symbolism of the *Ofrenda*

The *ofrenda* is the centerpiece of *Día de los Muertos* celebrations, and each element on the altar holds deep symbolic meaning. The marigold flower, known as *cempasúchil*, is believed to attract the spirits of the dead with its bright color and strong fragrance. Candles are lit to guide the spirits on their journey, while incense made from copal is burned to purify the space and create a sacred atmosphere.

Photos of the deceased are placed on the altar, along with their favorite foods and drinks, as it is believed that the spirits can enjoy the essence of these offerings. *Pan de muerto* (bread of the dead), a sweet bread often shaped like bones, is a traditional offering, as are sugar skulls, which are intricately decorated and often bear the names of the deceased.

The Festive Spirit of *Día de los Muertos*

In addition to the *ofrendas*, *Día de los Muertos* is marked by public celebrations, including parades, music, and dance. People paint their faces as *calaveras* (skulls) and dress in elaborate costumes, symbolizing the idea that death is a natural part of life. Parades often feature giant skeleton puppets and floats decorated with marigolds and candles.

One of the most famous *Día de los Muertos* celebrations takes place in Oaxaca, where the streets come alive with music, processions, and stunning displays of altars. Families gather at cemeteries to clean and decorate the graves of their loved ones, sharing stories, food, and memories. The cemetery becomes a lively gathering place, filled with the sounds of laughter, song, and celebration.

Día de los Muertos in Popular Culture

In recent years, *Día de los Muertos* has gained international recognition, thanks in part to films like *Coco* and *The Book of Life*, which highlight the beauty and significance of the festival. While these portrayals have helped bring attention to the holiday, they also emphasize the importance of understanding and respecting the cultural context of *Día de los Muertos*.

The festival is not simply a "Mexican Halloween" but a deeply spiritual and meaningful tradition that celebrates life, honors the dead, and reinforces the idea that death is a natural and inevitable part of existence.

Halloween may have originated in the Celtic lands of Europe, but its influence has spread far and wide, inspiring a diverse array of traditions and celebrations around the world. From the spooky revelry of American Halloween to the solemn rituals of *Día de los Muertos*, the holiday serves as a reminder of our shared fascination with death, the supernatural, and the unknown. Each culture's unique way of celebrating the dead reflects its beliefs, values, and history, creating a rich tapestry of global Halloween traditions that continue to evolve and captivate.

CHAPTER 7: FAMOUS HAUNTED LOCATIONS AROUND THE WORLD

The world is full of places that seem to carry the weight of their history—some that evoke feelings of awe and wonder, while others send shivers down our spines. Haunted locations are a fascinating subject, blending local legends, eerie tales, and paranormal investigations. These places are often sites of tragedy or mystery, where past events seem to echo into the present, leaving an otherworldly mark that captivates those brave enough to visit. In this chapter, we will explore some of the most famous haunted locations from around the world, each with its own spine-tingling stories and paranormal encounters.

7.1 Most hunted place around the world

The Tower of London, England

The Tower of London, a historic fortress on the banks of the River Thames, has stood as a symbol of power and tragedy for nearly a thousand years. It is one of the most haunted places in England, with a dark history of executions, imprisonment, and betrayal.

A History of Death and Betrayal

The Tower of London's gruesome past began in 1078 when William the Conqueror built it as a royal palace and stronghold. Over the centuries, it became notorious as a prison, where many prominent figures met untimely deaths. The most famous of these is Anne Boleyn, the second wife of King Henry VIII, who was executed in 1536 on charges of adultery, treason, and incest. Visitors to the Tower have reported sightings of her ghost, walking headless through the halls where she once lived.

Other ghostly figures reportedly haunting the Tower include Lady Jane Grey, the nine-day queen who was executed in 1554, and the two young princes, Edward V and Richard, Duke of York, who were imprisoned and mysteriously disappeared, believed to have been murdered by their uncle, Richard III.

Ghostly Encounters

Over the centuries, there have been countless reports of strange occurrences at the Tower. Guards and visitors alike have reported hearing phantom footsteps, disembodied voices, and sudden cold spots. The ghost of Anne Boleyn is said to be one of the most frequently sighted, often appearing near the site of her execution or in the Chapel of St. Peter ad Vincula, where she is buried.

One of the most chilling tales involves the sighting of two small figures dressed in old-fashioned clothes, believed to be the ghosts of the two young princes. Their pale, sad faces are said to occasionally appear in the shadows, reminding visitors of the dark fate that befell them within the Tower's walls.

The Stanley Hotel, Colorado, USA

Nestled in the picturesque Rocky Mountains, the Stanley Hotel in Estes Park, Colorado, is known for its stunning views and elegant architecture. However, it is perhaps most famous for its paranormal activity and its connection to Stephen King's *The Shining*, which was inspired by a stay at the hotel.

A Haunted History

Built in 1909 by F.O. Stanley, the hotel was originally a luxury resort catering to wealthy visitors looking to enjoy the natural beauty of the Rockies. However, over the years, guests and staff began to report strange occurrences that seemed to suggest the hotel was home to more than just living visitors.

The most famous ghostly residents of the Stanley Hotel are F.O. Stanley himself and his wife, Flora. Guests have reported seeing Stanley's apparition in the hotel's lobby and billiard room, while Flora's ghost is said to play the piano in the ballroom. There are also reports of a child's laughter echoing through the halls and objects moving on their own.

Stephen King's Stay and *The Shining*

The Stanley Hotel's haunted reputation reached new heights after Stephen King stayed there in the 1970s. King and his wife were the only guests in the hotel at the time, and King had a vivid nightmare about his son being chased through the halls. This experience inspired him to write *The Shining*, one of his most famous horror novels.

Since the release of *The Shining*, the Stanley Hotel has become a popular destination for ghost hunters and horror fans alike. The hotel even offers ghost tours, where visitors can explore the most haunted areas, including Room 217, where King stayed, and the fourth floor, which is known for its high concentration of paranormal activity.

The Catacombs of Paris, France

Beneath the bustling streets of Paris lies a vast network of tunnels and caves known as the Catacombs. This underground ossuary is home to the remains of over six million people, their bones carefully arranged along the walls of the tunnels. It is a place of both historical significance and eerie mystery, drawing visitors from around the world who are intrigued by its dark atmosphere and chilling reputation.

A City of the Dead

The Catacombs were created in the late 18th century as a solution to the overflowing cemeteries of Paris. The remains of millions of Parisians were exhumed and transferred to the underground tunnels, where they were meticulously arranged in patterns and designs. The result is a macabre labyrinth of bones that stretches for miles beneath the city.

Despite being a popular tourist attraction, the Catacombs have long been associated with tales of hauntings and paranormal activity. Visitors report feeling uneasy as they wander through the dark, narrow tunnels, with many claiming to hear whispers, footsteps, and the feeling of being watched.

Paranormal Encounters

Over the years, numerous paranormal investigators have explored the Catacombs, and many have reported strange occurrences. Some claim to have seen shadowy figures moving through the tunnels, while others have captured ghostly apparitions on camera. One of the most famous stories involves a group of explorers who entered the Catacombs in the 1990s and found footage of a man who appeared to be lost in the tunnels. His body was never found, and the footage remains a mystery to this day.

The atmosphere of the Catacombs is undeniably eerie, and whether or not you believe in ghosts, it's hard to deny the sense of unease that pervades this underground city of the dead.

Poveglia Island, Italy

Located in the Venetian Lagoon, Poveglia Island is often referred to as one of the most haunted places in the world. Its dark history, which includes being used as a quarantine station during the plague and later as a mental hospital, has earned it a reputation as a place of suffering and torment.

A Dark Past

Poveglia's history is steeped in tragedy. During the Black Death, the island was used as a quarantine station for those infected with the plague. Thousands of people were sent to the island, where they were left to die. It is believed that the bodies of over 160,000 plague victims are buried on the island, their ashes still mixed with the soil.

In the 20th century, the island became the site of a mental hospital, where patients were subjected to cruel and inhumane treatments. According to local legend, a deranged doctor who performed lobotomies on the patients eventually went mad and threw himself from the hospital's bell tower. His ghost is said to haunt the island, along with the restless spirits of the plague victims.

Ghostly Activity

Due to its grim history, Poveglia Island is said to be haunted by the tortured souls of those who died there. Visitors have reported hearing screams, footsteps, and ghostly whispers, as well as seeing shadowy figures moving through the crumbling ruins of the hospital. The island is so infamous for its paranormal activity that it is often referred to as "the island of no return," as those who visit often feel an overwhelming sense of dread and are eager to leave as soon as possible.

Despite its haunted reputation, Poveglia remains a popular destination for paranormal enthusiasts, though it is officially off-limits to the public. Those who have managed to explore the island describe it as one of the most terrifying places they've ever visited.

The Myrtles Plantation, Louisiana, USA

The Myrtles Plantation, located in St. Francisville, Louisiana, is often referred to as one of the most haunted homes in America. Built in 1796, the plantation has a long and bloody history, filled with tales of murder, betrayal, and ghostly apparitions.

The Legend of Chloe

One of the most famous legends associated with the Myrtles Plantation is that of Chloe, a slave who is said to have poisoned the wife and children of the plantation's owner, Clark Woodruff. According to the story, Chloe was caught eavesdropping on a conversation and had her ear cut off as punishment. In retaliation, she poisoned a birthday cake meant for Woodruff's wife, Sara, and their children. The plan backfired, and both Sara and her daughters died. Chloe was hanged for her crime, and her ghost is said to haunt the plantation to this day.

Visitors to the Myrtles Plantation have reported seeing the ghostly figure of a woman wearing a green turban, believed to be Chloe, wandering the grounds. There are also reports of the sounds of children's laughter and the appearance of ghostly figures in the plantation's windows.

Other Paranormal Activity

In addition to Chloe's ghost, the Myrtles Plantation is said to be home to numerous other spirits. The plantation's grand piano is known to play on its own, and guests have reported hearing phantom footsteps and voices in empty rooms. Some visitors have even captured ghostly figures in photographs, adding to the plantation's eerie reputation.

Despite its haunted history, the Myrtles Plantation is now a bed and breakfast, where guests can spend the night and experience the paranormal activity for themselves. For those who are brave enough, the plantation offers ghost tours, allowing visitors to explore the most haunted areas of the property.

From the haunted halls of the Tower of London to the eerie tunnels of the Paris Catacombs, these famous locations around the world share a common thread of tragedy and mystery. Whether you believe in ghosts or not, the stories of these haunted places continue to captivate and intrigue, drawing visitors from far and wide who are eager to experience the paranormal for themselves. While some may find comfort in the idea that the spirits of the past still linger, others may be left with a lingering sense of unease, wondering what truly lies beyond the veil of death.

7.2 Real-Life Paranormal Encounters: Ghosts Among Us

Real-life paranormal encounters captivate people across the globe, inspiring fascination and fear in equal measure. While many ghost stories can be dismissed as mere folklore or the product of overactive imaginations, some experiences defy explanation, leaving even skeptics at a loss. From shadowy figures in the night to objects moving on their own, people from all walks of life have reported chilling encounters that suggest we may not be as alone as we think.

The Enfield Poltergeist: A Family Under Siege

One of the most well-known and widely documented paranormal cases in history is the Enfield Poltergeist, which took place in a small house in Enfield, North

London, during the late 1970s. This terrifying series of events became a worldwide sensation, captivating media attention and baffling investigators.

The Haunting Begins

In 1977, Peggy Hodgson, a single mother, reported strange disturbances in her home. Her daughters, Janet and Margaret, were the first to experience these bizarre occurrences. Furniture began moving on its own, knocking sounds were heard throughout the house, and objects would fly through the air seemingly at random. The situation escalated when Janet, the younger daughter, claimed she was being thrown from her bed by an unseen force.

Soon, the entire family witnessed terrifying events: doors slamming, heavy furniture being overturned, and even disembodied voices speaking. Janet, in particular, seemed to be the focal point of the haunting. A voice that claimed to be a deceased man named Bill Wilkins spoke through her, terrifying everyone involved.

Paranormal Investigators Get Involved

The case drew the attention of paranormal investigators, most notably Maurice Grosse and Guy Lyon Playfair from the Society for Psychical Research. They spent over a year documenting the events in the Hodgson home. Their findings included audio recordings of knocking sounds, the inexplicable movement of objects, and strange voices emanating from Janet. The investigators were convinced that the haunting was genuine, though skeptics later raised doubts about some of the events.

The Enfield Poltergeist remains one of the most famous paranormal cases in history and inspired various films, documentaries, and books, including *The Conjuring 2*. While some believe the family fabricated the story for attention, many of the events remain unexplained to this day.

The Brown Lady of Raynham Hall: A Ghostly Apparition Captured on Camera

Raynham Hall, a grand estate in Norfolk, England, is home to one of the most famous ghost photographs ever taken. Known as the Brown Lady of Raynham Hall, this mysterious apparition has been sighted numerous times over the centuries, but it was a single photograph taken in 1936 that solidified her place in paranormal history.

The Legend of the Brown Lady

The Brown Lady is said to be the spirit of Lady Dorothy Walpole, who lived in Raynham Hall during the early 18th century. According to local legend, Lady Dorothy was locked away in the hall by her husband after she was accused of infidelity. She remained there until her death in 1726. Since then, numerous visitors and residents have reported seeing her ghostly figure wandering the halls, dressed in a brown brocade gown.

The most famous sighting occurred in 1936, when photographers from *Country Life* magazine were taking pictures of the interior of Raynham Hall. As they were setting up their camera, they noticed a misty figure descending the main staircase. They quickly took a photograph, which later revealed a transparent, ghostly figure of a woman. The photograph, now known as the Brown Lady of Raynham Hall, has been studied and debated by paranormal investigators and skeptics alike. Many believe it to be one of the most compelling pieces of evidence for the existence of ghosts.

The Myrtles Plantation: A Southern Haunting

Located in Louisiana, the Myrtles Plantation is often referred to as one of the most haunted homes in America. Built in 1796, the plantation is steeped in history, including stories of murder, betrayal, and ghostly apparitions. Visitors to the plantation have reported countless paranormal encounters, from sightings of shadowy figures to inexplicable footsteps and voices.

The Ghost of Chloe

The most famous legend associated with the Myrtles Plantation is the story of Chloe, a slave who allegedly poisoned the wife and children of the plantation's owner. According to the story, Chloe was caught eavesdropping and had her ear cut off as punishment. In retaliation, she poisoned a birthday cake intended for the family, but the plan backfired, and the owner's wife and children died. Chloe was later hanged by her fellow slaves, and her ghost is said to haunt the plantation to this day.

Visitors often report seeing a woman in a green turban wandering the grounds, believed to be Chloe's restless spirit. The plantation's grand mirror is also said to trap the spirits of those who died within its walls. Guests have reported seeing faces and handprints appear in the mirror, despite it being cleaned regularly.

Other Hauntings

In addition to Chloe's ghost, the Myrtles Plantation is home to other spirits, including children who are heard laughing and playing in the halls. One of the most chilling stories involves a piano that plays by itself, often in the middle of the night, sending shivers down the spines of those who hear its eerie melody.

The Myrtles Plantation has been featured on several paranormal investigation shows, and it continues to draw visitors who are intrigued by its haunted reputation.

Whether or not you believe in ghosts, the eerie atmosphere of the plantation leaves a lasting impression on those who visit.

The Ghosts of Gettysburg: Spirits of the Battlefield

The Battle of Gettysburg, one of the bloodiest battles of the American Civil War, left behind a legacy of tragedy and loss. Thousands of soldiers died on the battlefield, and many believe that their spirits still linger in the area, unable to find peace. The town of Gettysburg, Pennsylvania, has become a hotspot for paranormal activity, with countless reports of ghostly encounters over the years.

Soldiers Still Roam the Battlefield

Visitors to Gettysburg often report seeing apparitions of soldiers dressed in Civil War uniforms, marching across the battlefield or standing guard as if the battle never ended. Some have heard the sound of gunfire, cannon blasts, and the clashing of swords, despite no re-enactments taking place. These spectral soldiers are said to appear at dawn or dusk, when the light is low and the fog creeps across the fields.

One of the most famous haunted locations in Gettysburg is the Devil's Den, a rocky outcropping where intense fighting took place during the battle. Many visitors report feeling an overwhelming sense of dread when they approach the area, and some have seen shadowy figures moving among the rocks.

Ghosts in the Historic Town

The town of Gettysburg itself is also known for its hauntings. Several buildings that served as makeshift hospitals during the battle are said to be haunted by the spirits of soldiers who died there. The Gettysburg Hotel, for instance, is reportedly haunted by the ghost of a Confederate soldier who roams the halls, as well as a woman in period clothing who appears in the ballroom.

Gettysburg's haunted reputation has made it a popular destination for ghost tours, where visitors can explore the most haunted sites and hear stories of paranormal encounters. The lingering presence of the past makes Gettysburg a unique and eerie place, where history and the supernatural intertwine.

The Reality of Paranormal Encounters

Real-life paranormal encounters are often met with skepticism, but for those who have experienced them firsthand, the fear and confusion are all too real. Whether these ghostly apparitions are spirits of the dead, residual energy from traumatic events, or simply the product of the human mind trying to make sense of the unknown, they remain a source of fascination and intrigue. As we explore the darker corners of history and the places where the line between the living and the dead seems to blur, we are reminded of the mysteries that still elude us—and the possibility that there is much more to the world than we can see.

7.3 Travel Guide: The Most Haunted Destinations for Halloween Adventures

Halloween is the perfect time to explore some of the world's most haunted destinations. For thrill-seekers and ghost enthusiasts, there is nothing quite like visiting places with dark, eerie pasts. These haunted locations offer the perfect combination of history, folklore, and spine-chilling atmospheres that make them ideal for a Halloween adventure.

1. Salem, Massachusetts: A Town with a Dark Past

No list of haunted destinations would be complete without mentioning Salem, Massachusetts. This small New England town is infamous for the Salem Witch Trials of 1692, during which 20 people were executed after being accused of witchcraft. The town's grim history has left a lasting mark, with many believing that the spirits of those who perished during the trials still linger.

Must-See Haunted Locations in Salem

- **The Witch House:** Once home to Judge Jonathan Corwin, who presided over the witch trials, this house is the only structure still standing in Salem with direct ties to the trials. Visitors report feeling cold spots and a heavy, oppressive energy inside.
- **The Old Burying Point Cemetery:** One of the oldest cemeteries in the United States, this burial ground is said to be haunted by the restless spirits of those involved in the trials.
- **The Joshua Ward House:** Built in the 18th century, this house sits on land once owned by Sheriff George Corwin, who played a significant role in the witch trials. It is rumored to be haunted by the spirit of Corwin himself, as well as several of the accused witches.

Halloween Activities in Salem

Salem fully embraces its haunted reputation, especially during October. The town hosts numerous events, including ghost tours, witchcraft museums, and reenactments of the trials. The city's month-long celebration, known as "Haunted Happenings," features costume parties, parades, and candlelit tours that take you deep into Salem's spooky past.

2. Edinburgh, Scotland: Ghosts of the Underground

Edinburgh is a city steeped in history, and much of that history is dark and unsettling. From plague-ridden streets to ancient burial grounds, the city is home to countless ghost stories. One of the most famous haunted spots in Edinburgh is the city's underground vaults, which were built in the late 18th century and have become a hotspot for paranormal activity.

Must-See Haunted Locations in Edinburgh

- **The Edinburgh Vaults:** Located beneath the South Bridge, these vaults were once home to some of the city's poorest residents and were the site of murders and criminal activity. Visitors have reported seeing shadowy figures, hearing disembodied voices, and feeling sudden temperature drops.
- **Greyfriars Kirkyard:** This ancient cemetery is said to be haunted by the spirit of Sir George Mackenzie, a notorious judge who persecuted hundreds of Covenanters in the 17th century. His ghost, known as the "Mackenzie Poltergeist," is believed to cause physical harm to those who visit his tomb.

- **Mary King's Close:** This underground street was sealed off during the plague in the 17th century, leaving its residents to die. It is now one of Edinburgh's most haunted sites, with reports of ghostly apparitions and eerie sounds echoing through the abandoned homes.

Halloween Activities in Edinburgh

Edinburgh's ghost tours are particularly popular around Halloween, with many offering late-night visits to the city's most haunted locations. You can also visit the Edinburgh Dungeon, where actors bring the city's darkest history to life, or attend one of the many Halloween-themed events that take place in the city's historic Old Town.

3. New Orleans, Louisiana: A City of Spirits and Voodoo

New Orleans is famous for its vibrant culture, but it also has a darker side steeped in ghostly legends and voodoo practices. The French Quarter, with its historic architecture and cobblestone streets, is said to be home to numerous haunted locations, including hotels, cemeteries, and old mansions.

Must-See Haunted Locations in New Orleans

- **The LaLaurie Mansion:** This grand mansion in the French Quarter was once home to Madame Delphine LaLaurie, a wealthy socialite with a dark secret. After a fire broke out in the mansion, the bodies of tortured slaves were discovered in her attic, leading to rumors that their spirits still haunt the house today.
- **St. Louis Cemetery No. 1:** The oldest cemetery in New Orleans, St. Louis Cemetery No. 1 is the final resting place of many notable figures, including the famous voodoo queen Marie Laveau. Visitors claim to see her ghost wandering the cemetery, while others report strange rituals taking place near her tomb.
- **Hotel Monteleone:** This historic hotel is said to be haunted by several spirits, including a young boy who roams the hallways and a mysterious figure seen in the hotel's bar.

Halloween Activities in New Orleans

Halloween in New Orleans is a grand affair, with the city hosting parades, costume balls, and ghost tours throughout the month of October. The French Quarter is alive with spooky decorations, and many restaurants and bars offer themed drinks and dishes. For those interested in the city's voodoo history, a visit to one of the local voodoo shops or the Voodoo Museum is a must.

4. Bran Castle, Romania: The Legendary Home of Dracula

Bran Castle, located in the heart of Romania's Transylvania region, is often associated with the legend of Dracula, thanks to its eerie appearance and its ties to Vlad the Impaler, the brutal ruler who inspired Bram Stoker's famous vampire character. While it's uncertain whether Vlad ever lived in the castle, its remote location, dark history, and Gothic architecture make it the perfect setting for a Halloween adventure.

Must-See Haunted Locations at Bran Castle

- **The Castle Itself:** Bran Castle's towering walls and labyrinthine corridors have given rise to numerous ghost stories. Some visitors claim to hear footsteps echoing through the halls or feel an unsettling presence watching them as they explore the castle.
- **Poenari Fortress:** For those looking to delve deeper into the Dracula legend, a visit to the nearby Poenari Fortress is a must. This crumbling ruin was once a stronghold of Vlad the Impaler, and many believe his spirit still haunts the site.

Halloween Activities at Bran Castle

Every year, Bran Castle hosts a special Halloween event, where visitors can explore the castle at night and enjoy a party in the courtyard. Guests are encouraged to dress in costume, and the event features live music, food, and drinks. It's a once-in-a-lifetime opportunity to experience Halloween in the home of the world's most famous vampire.

5. The Tower of London, England: A Fortress of Fear

The Tower of London has a long and bloody history, having served as a royal palace, prison, and execution site over the centuries. It's no surprise that this imposing fortress is considered one of the most haunted places in England. The spirits of those who were executed or imprisoned within its walls are said to still roam the grounds, with visitors reporting ghostly apparitions, strange sounds, and an overwhelming sense of dread.

Must-See Haunted Locations in the Tower of London

- **The White Tower:** This central keep is said to be haunted by the ghost of Anne Boleyn, the second wife of King Henry VIII, who was executed at the Tower in 1536. Her headless spirit has been seen wandering the grounds, particularly near the spot where she was beheaded.
- **The Bloody Tower:** The Bloody Tower is infamous for the mysterious disappearance of the

two young princes, Edward V and his brother Richard. Their spirits are believed to haunt the tower, with some visitors reporting the sound of children crying late at night.

Halloween Activities at the Tower of London

While the Tower of London is not specifically known for Halloween events, its year-round ghost tours provide a spooky experience for those looking to delve into the site's haunted history. Visitors can explore the tower's many rooms and hear stories of the executions, murders, and ghostly encounters that have taken place over the centuries.

Planning Your Haunted Halloween Adventure

Whether you're looking for ghostly thrills or a deeper connection to history, these haunted destinations offer a perfect blend of both. From the witch trials of Salem to the haunted vaults of Edinburgh, each location has its own unique story to tell, making them ideal spots for a Halloween adventure. As you plan your trip, be sure to pack your courage—you never know what you might encounter on your journey into the paranormal.

CHAPTER 8: HALLOWEEN FOR KIDS

8.1 Safe Trick-or-Treating Tips for Parents

Halloween is one of the most exciting holidays for kids, filled with candy, costumes, and the thrill of trick-or-treating. But it's also a time when parents need to be extra vigilant to ensure their children stay safe while having fun. With the right planning, communication, and safety measures, parents can help their kids enjoy Halloween traditions without unnecessary risks. This section will cover a range of essential tips for safe trick-or-treating, including costume safety, road awareness, candy checks, and the importance of staying together.

1. Plan Ahead for a Safe and Fun Halloween

Before you head out on Halloween night, it's essential to have a plan. This involves picking a safe neighborhood, setting clear guidelines for your kids, and ensuring everyone knows what to expect. Preparation can make a significant difference in how smoothly the night goes.

Choosing a Safe Trick-or-Treating Route

- **Stick to Familiar Areas:** Choose a neighborhood where you feel comfortable and that you know well. Ideally, this should be a well-lit area with sidewalks and minimal traffic.
- **Check Local Events:** Some communities offer organized trick-or-treating events or block parties where the streets are closed to traffic, making it safer for kids to go from house to house. Many schools, churches, and community centers also offer trunk-or-treat events, where kids can collect candy in a safe environment.
- **Create a Route Map:** Before heading out, plan a route that avoids busy streets and unlit areas. Keep your route short enough for young children to handle and make sure it loops back to your starting point.

Setting Clear Expectations with Kids

- **Stay Together:** Remind your children to stick with their group and not wander off alone, even if they see friends or are tempted by a particularly inviting house. Consider using a buddy system where each child has a partner to ensure no one gets separated.
- **Establish a Return Time:** If your older children are trick-or-treating without you, set a specific time for them to return home and make sure they have a phone or a way to contact you if needed.
- **No Eating Candy Until You're Home:** Explain to your kids that while collecting candy is fun, they should wait until they get home to eat any treats. This will allow you to check for any potential hazards (we'll cover candy safety later on).

2. Costume Safety: Comfort, Visibility, and Fire Resistance

Costumes are one of the most exciting parts of Halloween for kids, but they can also pose safety risks if not chosen carefully. Parents should ensure that costumes are not only fun and creative but also safe and comfortable for walking in the dark.

Visibility Is Key

- **Use Bright or Reflective Materials:** Dark costumes are common, especially for spooky characters like witches, vampires, and skeletons. However, dark clothing can make children less visible to drivers. Consider adding reflective tape or glow-in-the-dark accessories to your child's costume to increase visibility.
- **Glow Sticks and Flashlights:** Equip your child with a glow stick or a small flashlight to carry while trick-or-treating. These not only help your child see where they're going but also make them more visible to others.

Comfortable and Well-Fitting Costumes

- **Avoid Tripping Hazards:** Make sure that costumes are not too long and that your child can walk comfortably without tripping. Hem any costumes that drag on the ground, and opt for comfortable shoes rather than costume footwear that may be difficult to walk in.
- **Properly Fitting Masks and Headgear:** Masks can obstruct vision and make it harder for children to see oncoming traffic or obstacles in their path. Consider using face paint instead of masks, or ensure that the mask has large enough eye holes to see clearly. Additionally, headgear

such as hats or helmets should fit snugly but not restrict vision or movement.

- **Weather-Appropriate Costumes:** Consider the weather when choosing a costume. If it's cold, make sure your child can wear warm clothing underneath their costume or bring along a jacket. On the other hand, if it's warm, ensure the costume is breathable and lightweight to prevent overheating.

Fire-Resistant Materials

- **Choose Flame-Retardant Costumes:** Many Halloween decorations, such as jack-o'-lanterns and candles, involve open flames. Make sure your child's costume is made from flame-resistant materials to reduce the risk of accidents. Check the costume labels or packaging for flame-retardant materials before purchasing.

3. Trick-or-Treating Road Safety

Children are often excited and distracted while trick-or-treating, which can increase the risk of accidents on the road. Parents need to be proactive in teaching their children about road safety, especially when walking in the dark.

Staying on the Sidewalks

- **Walk, Don't Run:** Encourage your children to walk, not run, from house to house. Running increases the risk of tripping, falling, or darting out into the street without looking.
- **Use Sidewalks:** Stay on the sidewalks as much as possible. If your neighborhood doesn't have sidewalks, walk on the left side of the road, facing traffic, so you can see oncoming cars.
- **Crossing the Street Safely:** Teach your children to cross the street at designated crosswalks or intersections. Make sure they look both ways before crossing and remind them to hold an adult's hand or stay with their group.

Drivers on Halloween Night

- **Increased Traffic Awareness:** Halloween night is busier than usual, with more cars on the road and excited trick-or-treaters crossing streets. Drivers may be distracted, and kids may not always pay attention, so it's essential to be extra vigilant.
- **Stay Alert Near Driveways:** Remind children to be cautious around parked cars and driveways, as drivers may not see them when backing out.

4. Checking Candy for Safety

One of the most iconic aspects of Halloween is the abundance of candy that kids collect. However, not all treats are safe to eat immediately. Parents should always inspect their children's candy haul before allowing them to dig in, especially if they're trick-or-treating in unfamiliar neighborhoods.

Inspecting Candy

- **Check for Tampering:** Look for any signs of tampering, such as torn wrappers, loose packaging, or anything that looks unusual. If a candy wrapper is punctured, unsealed, or homemade, it's best to discard it to be safe.
- **Avoid Homemade Treats:** Unless you personally know the person who made the homemade treat, it's safer to avoid consuming any homemade goods collected during trick-or-treating.
- **Be Wary of Unlabeled Items:** Some candies, especially small or novelty items, may not have proper labeling. If you're unsure about an item's ingredients or packaging, it's better to discard it.

Allergy Awareness

- **Watch for Allergens:** For children with food allergies, Halloween can be especially tricky. Make sure to check labels for common allergens like peanuts, tree nuts, dairy, soy, and gluten. Many candy manufacturers now provide allergen information on packaging, but if the label is unclear, it's safer to avoid giving it to your child.
- **Teal Pumpkin Project:** Consider participating in the Teal Pumpkin Project, which encourages homes to offer non-food treats for trick-or-treaters with allergies. Placing a teal pumpkin outside your home signals to kids with food allergies that you have safe, non-edible treats available, such as stickers, small toys, or glow sticks.

5. Staying Together: The Importance of Supervision

For younger children, supervision is key to ensuring a safe and enjoyable trick-or-treating experience. Even older children should be given guidelines and check-in points to ensure they stay safe while out on their own.

Supervising Young Children

- **Adult Supervision:** If your children are young, it's best to accompany them while they trick-or-treat. Not only does this provide an extra layer of safety, but it also allows you to share in the fun and keep an eye on them as they explore the neighborhood.

- **Group Trick-or-Treating:** Encourage trick-or-treating in groups. Whether with family or friends, sticking together helps ensure that no one gets lost or left behind.

Safe Alternatives to Traditional Trick-or-Treating

- **Trunk-or-Treat Events:** Many communities, schools, and churches now offer trunk-or-treat events as a safer alternative to traditional trick-or-treating. These events usually take place in a parking lot, where cars are decorated and filled with candy, offering a safe, supervised environment for children to collect treats.
- **Halloween Parties:** Consider hosting a Halloween party or attending one in place of trick-or-treating. This allows children to enjoy the festivities in a controlled and safe environment while still wearing costumes and enjoying treats.

Making Halloween Safe and Fun for All Ages

Halloween is a magical time for kids, and with a little extra preparation and safety awareness, it can be a fun and memorable experience for the whole family. By choosing safe costumes, planning a well-lit route, staying vigilant on the roads, and checking candy for hazards, parents can ensure their children enjoy trick-or-treating to the fullest. Safety doesn't have to take away from the excitement—it only enhances the fun by giving kids and parents peace of mind.

8.2   Family-Friendly   Halloween Games and Activities

Halloween is a special time of year when families can come together to create lasting memories filled with laughter, creativity, and, of course, a little spookiness. While trick-or-treating is often the highlight of the evening, there are many other ways to celebrate the holiday with fun, family-friendly games and activities. From classic Halloween party games to creative DIY activities.

1. Classic Halloween Games for Kids

When it comes to Halloween, traditional games are always a hit. These classic games are easy to set up and adapt to a Halloween theme, making them perfect for family gatherings, school parties, or neighborhood events.

1.1 Bobbing for Apples

One of the most iconic Halloween games is bobbing for apples, a simple yet timeless activity that dates back centuries. Traditionally played at harvest festivals, bobbing for apples involves filling a large basin with water and floating apples on the surface. Participants must then try to catch an apple using only their mouths—no hands allowed!

How to Play:

- Fill a large tub or basin with water and place several apples in it. Make sure the apples float freely.
- Each player takes turns trying to grab an apple using their mouth, with hands behind their back.
- The first person to successfully bite into an apple wins.

  Variations for Younger Kids:
- Use smaller apples or soft balls for younger children to make it easier.
- If you're concerned about hygiene or sharing water, you can hang apples from strings and have kids try to bite into them while they dangle.

1.2 Pin the Hat on the Witch

A Halloween twist on the classic "Pin the Tail on the Donkey," this game is simple to organize and always brings lots of giggles.

How to Play:

- Draw or print out a large picture of a witch without her hat and tape it to the wall.
- Cut out a paper hat for each participant, making sure to put each person's name on the hat.
- Blindfold the players one at a time and have them try to pin (or tape) the hat on the witch's head. Whoever gets the hat closest to the correct spot wins.

  Variations:
- You can change the theme to "Pin the Nose on the Pumpkin" or "Pin the Spider on the Web" for a creative twist.
- For younger kids, you can skip the blindfold to make it easier.

1.3 Mummy Wrap

This game is a fantastic way to get kids excited and involved, and it's as simple as it is entertaining.

How to Play:

- Divide the kids into teams of two or three.
- Give each team a roll of toilet paper or crepe paper streamers.

- One person from each team is chosen to be the "mummy," while the others wrap them up from head to toe (leaving space for the face).
- The first team to successfully wrap their mummy wins, or you can judge the best-looking mummy.
  Tips for Fun:
- Make it a timed challenge—see who can wrap the mummy the fastest in one or two minutes.
- Be sure to take lots of pictures of the wrapped mummies for some silly memories!

1.4 Pumpkin Bowling

If you're looking for an activity that combines fun with a bit of skill, pumpkin bowling is an excellent choice. It's a twist on regular bowling, but with small pumpkins instead of bowling balls and plastic bottles instead of pins.

How to Play:

- Set up six or more empty plastic bottles or cans as bowling pins in a triangle formation.
- Give each player a small pumpkin to use as a bowling ball.
- Have players take turns rolling the pumpkin toward the pins, trying to knock them over.
- Keep score just like in a regular bowling game, with each player getting two rolls per turn.
  Fun Variations:

- Paint the bottles with spooky faces or wrap them in white tape to look like mummies.
- Instead of using pumpkins, you can also use round gourds or balls painted to look like pumpkins.

2. Crafty Halloween Activities

Halloween isn't just about candy and games—it's also a fantastic opportunity to get crafty and creative with DIY projects that kids and adults alike will love. Here are a few easy and fun crafts that make perfect family activities.

2.1 DIY Spooky Slime

Slime has been a popular craft for kids in recent years, and Halloween is the perfect time to make it even more fun by adding spooky elements.

How to Make It:

- **Ingredients:** Elmer's glue, baking soda, contact lens solution, and food coloring.
- Mix 1/2 cup of glue with a few drops of food coloring (orange, green, or purple works well for Halloween).
- Add 1/4 teaspoon of baking soda and mix.

- Add 1 tablespoon of contact lens solution and stir until it starts to form slime. If it's too sticky, add a bit more contact lens solution.
- To make it spookier, add plastic spiders, googly eyes, or glitter to the slime for extra Halloween flair.

Tips:

- This is a great activity to let kids be hands-on and get a little messy. Just make sure you have a washable surface to work on!

2.2 Halloween Mask-Making

Crafting your own Halloween masks is a fun and creative way for kids to express themselves. This activity is perfect for family time or as a party craft station.

How to Make It:

- Provide blank masks (available at most craft stores) or cut out mask shapes from cardboard.
- Set out materials like markers, paint, glue, feathers, glitter, and stickers so that kids can decorate their masks however they like.
- If you want to make it more Halloween-themed, offer shapes for monsters, ghosts, or pumpkins.
- Attach elastic or string to the sides of the mask so that kids can wear their creations when they're finished.

Encouraging Creativity:

- You can make this into a contest by awarding prizes for the scariest, funniest, or most creative masks.
- If you're hosting a Halloween party, the masks can double as part of the costume for the night.

2.3 Paper Plate Pumpkins

Paper plate crafts are always a hit with younger children, and making pumpkin faces is a simple and fun way to celebrate Halloween.

How to Make It:

- Give each child a plain white paper plate.
- Provide orange paint, markers, or crayons for coloring the plate like a pumpkin.
- Once the plate is colored, kids can cut out or glue on shapes for the eyes, nose, and mouth to create their own jack-o'-lantern faces.
- For added creativity, offer green paper or pipe cleaners for the pumpkin stem and leaves.
  Why It's Great:
- This craft is easy enough for young kids but still fun for older ones to get creative with different jack-o'-lantern designs.

3. Outdoor Halloween Games and Challenges

If the weather permits, take the Halloween fun outside with these active games and challenges that are sure to get the whole family involved.

3.1 Witch Hat Ring Toss

This simple game is perfect for outdoor Halloween parties and can be adapted for any age.
How to Play:

- Set up several plastic witch hats in a line or triangle on the ground.
- Use glow-in-the-dark rings or hoops (or even glow stick bracelets) and have players stand a few feet back.
- The goal is to toss the rings and try to land them on the pointy tops of the witch hats.
- Award points for each successful toss and offer small prizes for the winners.
  How to Make It:
- You can create your own witch hats by using black construction paper or cardstock. Simply roll the paper into a cone shape and secure it with tape or glue.

3.2 Halloween Scavenger Hunt

A Halloween scavenger hunt is a fantastic way to keep kids moving while also engaging their brains. This can be done in your backyard or even indoors.

How to Play:

- Create a list of Halloween-themed items for kids to find, such as plastic spiders, small pumpkins, black cats, bats, witches, or ghost cutouts.
- Hide these items around the yard or house and give each child or team a list to check off as they find each item.
- You can also provide clues or riddles for each item to make the game more challenging.

  Customizing the Game:
- For younger kids, keep it simple by using easy-to-find items. For older kids, make the clues more complex and hide items in tricky locations.
- Offer small prizes or candy to each participant as they finish the hunt.

3.3 Ghost Bowling

Much like pumpkin bowling, ghost bowling is an easy outdoor activity that can be played with minimal materials.

How to Play:

- Use empty cans or white plastic bottles and draw ghost faces on them with a marker.
- Stack the ghost cans or bottles in a pyramid formation.

- Use a small ball (you can paint it to look like a pumpkin) and let the kids take turns knocking down the ghost pins.
- Score it like regular bowling, with each player getting two chances to knock down as many ghosts as possible.

4. Halloween-Themed Story Time

Halloween is the perfect time for storytelling, whether it's spooky or silly. Storytime is an excellent way to wind down after a day of activities or as a quiet party station.

4.1 Telling Spooky Stories

For families who enjoy a little thrill, gather around with flashlights or lanterns and tell spooky (but not too scary) stories.

- You can make up your own ghost stories or read from classic children's books like *"The Little Old Lady Who Was Not Afraid of Anything"* or *"Room on the Broom."*
- Encourage kids to create their own spooky tales and share them with the group.
  Setting the Mood:
- Dim the lights or go outside with lanterns or candles to set the Halloween atmosphere.

- You can also add sound effects like creaking doors, howling winds, or rattling chains to make the stories even more immersive.

4.2 Halloween Charades

Charades is always a hit with kids, and giving it a Halloween theme adds a spooky twist. **How to Play:**

- Write down Halloween-related characters or activities on slips of paper, such as "ghost," "witch," "pumpkin carving," or "trick-or-treating."
- Divide the group into teams, and one player from each team acts out the word or phrase while their teammates try to guess what it is.
- Set a time limit for guessing, and whichever team has the most correct answers wins.

Fun for All Ages

The most important thing about Halloween is spending time with loved ones and creating happy memories. By incorporating these family-friendly games and activities into your Halloween celebration, you're sure to make the holiday even more special for everyone involved. Whether you're hosting a party or just looking for ways to keep the kids entertained at home, these games and crafts provide endless opportunities for fun, laughter, and creativity.

From the simple joy of crafting pumpkin faces to the excitement of a scavenger hunt, Halloween offers a chance to bring imagination to life. And remember, the best part of any holiday is the time spent together as a family.

8.3 DIY Costumes for Kids: Fun, Easy, and Affordable

One of the most exciting aspects of Halloween for kids is the chance to dress up in fun, imaginative costumes. While store-bought costumes can be convenient, creating DIY costumes at home adds a personal touch, making the holiday even more special. Crafting costumes at home can also be a budget-friendly option, allowing parents to get creative without breaking the bank. These costumes can be put together with common household items, basic crafting supplies, and a dash of imagination.

1. Why Choose DIY Costumes?

Before diving into specific costume ideas, let's first explore the benefits of choosing DIY over store-bought options.

1.1 Creativity and Individuality

One of the biggest advantages of making a costume at home is the ability to customize it exactly to your child's preferences. Store-bought costumes can be limited in style, size, and uniqueness, but a DIY costume offers limitless possibilities. Whether your child wants to be a classic character like a witch or a more unique creation like a "space unicorn," DIY costumes give you the flexibility to make something one-of-a-kind.

1.2 Cost-Effectiveness

Halloween costumes can get pricey, especially if you're buying for more than one child. DIY costumes allow you to save money by using materials you already have at home or purchasing inexpensive supplies. Many costumes can be created with items like old clothes, cardboard, fabric scraps, and craft supplies, making it easy to stay within budget.

1.3 Quality Time Together

Creating a costume at home can be a wonderful bonding activity for parents and kids. From brainstorming ideas to gathering materials and assembling the costume, the process provides a chance to work together and spend quality time. Kids will take pride in wearing something they helped create, making the experience even more meaningful.

1.4 Sustainable and Eco-Friendly

In today's world, sustainability is a growing concern. Instead of contributing to fast fashion and disposable costumes, DIY outfits can repurpose old clothing or materials, reducing waste. By using recyclable or reusable items, you're also teaching kids the value of sustainability and creativity.

2. Simple DIY Costume Ideas for Kids

Now that we've discussed the benefits of DIY costumes, let's dive into some fun and easy ideas that you can create at home with minimal time and effort.

2.1 Superhero Cape and Mask

Every child loves pretending to be a superhero, and with this simple DIY costume, they can become their favorite hero or invent their own unique character.
Materials Needed:

- Old t-shirt or fabric for the cape
- Felt or construction paper for the mask
- String or elastic for the mask
- Scissors, fabric glue, or a needle and thread

How to Make It:

1. **Cape:** Cut out the back of an old t-shirt to create a simple cape. Alternatively, you can use any piece of fabric you have at home, such as a pillowcase. Attach Velcro or tie strings to the top to secure it around the neck.
2. **Mask:** Cut out a mask shape from felt or construction paper and poke holes on either side. Attach string or elastic to the mask so it can be worn around the head.
3. **Emblem:** For an extra touch, you can cut out a superhero emblem from fabric or paper and glue it to the back of the cape. This could be a lightning bolt, star, or your child's initial.

Why It's Great:

- Super easy and quick to make
- Can be customized with different colors and symbols
- Comfortable for kids to wear during parties or while trick-or-treating

2.2 Animal Ears and Tail

For a cute and simple costume, transform your child into their favorite animal with just a few easy accessories: ears and a tail. Whether they want to be a cat, dog, bunny, or even a dinosaur, this costume can be adapted for different animals.

Materials Needed:

- Felt or fabric in appropriate colors
- Headband
- Stuffing (cotton or fabric scraps) for the tail
- Hot glue gun or fabric glue

How to Make It:

1. **Ears:** Cut ear shapes from felt or fabric in the color of the chosen animal. Use hot glue to attach the ears to a headband. For animals like cats or dogs, you can bend the ears to give them a more lifelike shape.
2. **Tail:** Cut out a long strip of fabric, sew or glue it into a tube, and stuff it with cotton or fabric scraps. Attach the tail to your child's waistband with a safety pin or by sewing it onto a belt loop.
3. **Face Paint:** Use face paint to draw whiskers, a nose, or other features to complete the look.

Why It's Great:

- Quick and affordable to make
- Comfortable and easy to wear
- Can be adapted for a variety of animals

2.3 Ghost Costume

The classic ghost costume never goes out of style and is one of the easiest costumes to make at home. It's perfect for kids who want to be spooky without much fuss.

Materials Needed:

- White bed sheet or large piece of fabric
- Scissors
- Black felt or fabric for eyes and mouth

How to Make It:

1. Cut out holes for your child's eyes and mouth on the sheet, making sure they're large enough for visibility and breathing.
2. Use black felt or fabric to create ghostly eyes and a mouth, and glue them onto the front of the sheet for a spooky effect.
3. Drape the sheet over your child, and you're done!

Why It's Great:

- Simple and classic
- Requires minimal materials and effort
- Can be made spooky or cute depending on how you style the face

2.4 Scarecrow

A scarecrow costume is not only easy to put together, but it's also great for fall festivals and Halloween. Plus, it has a fun and rustic charm that kids will love.

Materials Needed:

- Flannel shirt
- Overalls or jeans
- Straw (or raffia)
- Face paint
- Hat

How to Make It:

1. Dress your child in a flannel shirt and overalls or jeans.
2. Use straw or raffia to create the "stuffing." You can tuck pieces of straw into the sleeves, pant legs, and around the neckline.
3. Paint a scarecrow face with face paint—draw stitches on the mouth and nose for a classic scarecrow look.
4. Top it off with a straw hat, and your scarecrow is ready to go.

Why It's Great:

- Cozy and warm for chilly Halloween nights

- Easy to put together with clothes you already have at home
- Can be made as simple or detailed as you like

2.5 Pirate

Ahoy, matey! A pirate costume is a favorite for many kids and can be easily created with a few household items and some piratey accessories.

Materials Needed:

- Striped shirt or plain white t-shirt
- Black pants or leggings
- Bandana or eye patch
- Toy sword (optional)

How to Make It:

1. Dress your child in a striped shirt or plain t-shirt and black pants or leggings.
2. Tie a bandana around their head and use makeup or face paint to give them a pirate beard or mustache.
3. If you have a toy sword or a cardboard cutout, this can be the finishing touch for a swashbuckling pirate look.

Why It's Great:

- Easy to assemble with clothes you already own
- A popular costume choice with lots of creative potential
- Can be customized with accessories like toy swords, hooks, or a stuffed parrot

3. No-Sew Costume Ideas

If you don't have access to a sewing machine or just want to avoid sewing altogether, here are some fun and easy no-sew costume ideas.

3.1 Jellyfish Costume

This whimsical costume is not only easy to make, but it's also a great way to stand out in a crowd.

Materials Needed:

- Clear umbrella
- Blue or purple streamers or ribbons
- Hot glue or tape
- LED lights (optional)

How to Make It:

1. Attach blue, purple, or white streamers or ribbons to the edges of the umbrella to resemble jellyfish tentacles. You can use hot glue or tape to secure them.

2. If you want to add a glowing effect, attach battery-operated LED lights to the inside of the umbrella.
3. Your child can carry the umbrella and pretend to float along as a jellyfish.

Why It's Great:

- Eye-catching and creative
- Can be made with very few materials
- Perfect for a unique, non-spooky costume

3.2 Robot Costume

A DIY robot costume can be made with items you likely already have around the house. This costume is both fun to make and wear, giving kids a futuristic and playful look.

Materials Needed:

- Cardboard boxes (one for the body, one for the head)
- Silver spray paint or aluminum foil
- Bottle caps or buttons for controls
- Duct tape

How to Make It:

1. Cut holes for arms, legs, and the head in the larger box. Use a smaller box for the head, cutting out holes for eyes and the mouth.
2. Paint the boxes silver or cover them in aluminum foil to give the costume a metallic look.
3. Glue bottle caps, buttons, or other small items onto the chest box to create the robot's control panel.
4. Use duct tape to add extra details, like joints or wires.

Why It's Great:

- Kids love pretending to be robots!
- Very affordable, using mostly recycled materials
- A creative and out-of-the-box (literally) idea

4. Customizing DIY Costumes

One of the joys of making a DIY costume is the ability to personalize it and make it exactly how your child wants it. You can tweak any of these ideas to match your child's vision by changing colors, adding unique details, or incorporating their favorite accessories. Here are a few ways to customize DIY costumes for even more fun:

4.1 Add Glitter or Paint

If your child loves sparkles, consider adding glitter to their costume. You can apply fabric glue to areas of the costume and sprinkle glitter over the top. If glitter isn't their style, fabric paint is another great option for adding personalized designs.

4.2 Mix and Match Themes

Can't decide between a few costume ideas? Mix and match to create a hybrid costume! A pirate-witch or superhero-ghost can combine elements from multiple costumes for an even more creative and fun result.

4.3 Accessorize with Props

Props like a wizard's wand, a cowboy's lasso, or a fairy's wings can take a simple costume to the next level. If you're feeling crafty, you can make these props at home using materials like cardboard, paint, and fabric.

Halloween Magic on a Budget

DIY costumes are a fantastic way to celebrate Halloween in a creative, affordable, and personalized way. With a little imagination, you can transform everyday household items into magical costumes that your child will love. Not only will these costumes stand out, but they will also provide lasting memories of fun family time spent together.

By focusing on fun, easy, and affordable options, you can ensure that your Halloween costumes are a hit without adding stress or expense. Whether your child dreams of being a spooky ghost, a fearless superhero, or a lovable animal, the possibilities with DIY costumes are endless.

CHAPTER 9: INCLUSIVE HALLOWEEN CELEBRATIONS

9.1 Celebrating Halloween with Inclusivity and Accessibility

Halloween is a time for fun, creativity, and community spirit. It's a celebration that brings people together, whether it's for trick-or-treating, haunted houses, or festive parties. However, to ensure everyone feels included in the excitement, it's important to recognize that Halloween celebrations can present challenges for individuals with disabilities, allergies, or different cultural backgrounds. Creating an inclusive and accessible Halloween allows everyone, regardless of their abilities or needs, to fully enjoy the holiday in a way that's safe, respectful, and fun.

In this chapter, we'll explore ways to make Halloween more inclusive by addressing physical accessibility, food allergies, sensory sensitivities, and cultural considerations. We'll also look at tips and resources for parents, communities, and event organizers to create welcoming spaces for all participants.

1. Understanding the Importance of Inclusivity on Halloween

Inclusivity means ensuring that every child or individual has the opportunity to participate in the fun of Halloween. While most kids may have no trouble navigating the typical festivities, some may face barriers due to disabilities, dietary restrictions, or sensory sensitivities. Recognizing and addressing these barriers can transform the holiday experience for many, turning what might have been an isolating event into a joyful celebration for everyone.

1.1 Breaking Down Barriers

For children with disabilities, both physical and cognitive, traditional Halloween activities such as trick-or-treating or participating in group games can present significant challenges. Sidewalks and stairs might be difficult to navigate for those in wheelchairs, loud noises and flashing lights can overwhelm individuals with sensory processing issues, and non-verbal children may find it hard to participate in the same ways as their peers.

1.2 Creating a Welcoming Environment

An inclusive Halloween isn't just about adjusting logistics—it's also about fostering an environment where every child feels welcome, regardless of their differences. This involves educating others about the importance of inclusivity and encouraging neighbors, friends, and event organizers to take small steps to make sure everyone can join in on the fun.

1.3 Building Community and Empathy

Inclusive celebrations help build stronger, more compassionate communities. By considering the needs of others, we cultivate empathy, showing that Halloween can be a time not only for scares and treats but also for kindness and connection. When every child and family is able to take part in the holiday, it creates a sense of unity and shared joy that benefits the entire community.

2. Making Trick-or-Treating Accessible

Trick-or-treating is one of the most iconic Halloween traditions, but for children with disabilities, food allergies, or other challenges, it can be difficult to fully participate. By taking a few simple steps, you can ensure that your home and neighborhood are more accessible and welcoming to all trick-or-treaters.

2.1 Physical Accessibility for Trick-or-Treaters

For children with mobility issues, stairs, uneven sidewalks, and narrow pathways can create barriers to participating in trick-or-treating. To make sure that all children can approach your home and enjoy the experience of collecting candy, consider the following tips:

- **Use Ramps:** If you have stairs leading up to your front door, consider setting up a temporary ramp or handing out candy from a table set up at the bottom of your driveway or yard.
- **Clear Pathways:** Make sure your yard or driveway is free from obstacles like decorations, hoses, or uneven surfaces that could pose challenges for kids using wheelchairs or walkers.
- **Alternative Treating Areas:** If your neighborhood has homes that are hard to access, consider organizing a central trick-or-treating spot in a flat, open area like a park or community center, where kids of all abilities can gather safely.

2.2 Sensory-Friendly Trick-or-Treating

For children with sensory sensitivities, loud noises, flashing lights, and crowded spaces can turn Halloween into an overwhelming experience. Sensory-friendly trick-or-treating environments can help these children feel more comfortable and included. Here's how you can create a sensory-friendly space:

- **Limit Sound Effects:** While spooky music and sound effects are fun for many, they can be overwhelming for some kids. Consider keeping noise levels low or providing a quieter, less stimulating area for trick-or-treaters who may be sensitive to loud sounds.
- **Use Non-Flashing Lights:** Flashing or strobe lights can trigger sensory overload or even seizures in children with certain neurological conditions. Instead, opt for soft, steady lighting to set the Halloween mood without causing distress.
- **Designate Quiet Times:** Some neighborhoods or events designate certain hours as sensory-friendly trick-or-treating times, where lights are dimmed, sounds are minimized, and there are fewer crowds. This provides a calmer, more relaxed environment for kids who need it.

2.3 Non-Verbal Trick-or-Treaters

Some children may not be able to say "trick or treat" due to non-verbal communication needs. A smile, gesture, or card that says "Trick or Treat" can easily substitute for words. Be mindful of this and ensure that you still engage warmly with non-verbal children, acknowledging their participation and making them feel included.

2.4 Teal Pumpkin Project for Food Allergies

Food allergies are a significant concern for many children during Halloween, as many popular candies contain allergens like peanuts, dairy, or gluten. The Teal Pumpkin Project is an initiative designed to make Halloween safer and more inclusive for children with food allergies by offering non-food treats.

How to Participate in the Teal Pumpkin Project:

- **Display a Teal Pumpkin:** A teal-colored pumpkin outside your door signals to families that you are offering non-food treats for children with allergies.
- **Provide Non-Food Treats:** Stock up on inexpensive non-food items such as stickers, glow sticks, small toys, or temporary tattoos. These treats are safe for all children and provide an exciting alternative to candy.
- **Separate Treats:** If you're offering both candy and non-food treats, keep them in separate containers to avoid cross-contamination. Make it clear that children with allergies can safely choose the non-food options.

3. Inclusive Halloween Games and Activities

Whether you're hosting a Halloween party or participating in a school or community event, it's important to make sure that games and activities are designed with inclusivity in mind. This means considering the needs of children with disabilities, sensory sensitivities, and other special requirements to ensure everyone can participate and have fun.

3.1 Wheelchair-Friendly Games

Many traditional Halloween games, such as sack races or bobbing for apples, may not be accessible for children with mobility issues. Fortunately, there are plenty of ways to adapt games so that all children, including those using wheelchairs, can participate.

- **Pumpkin Bowling:** Set up a bowling game using lightweight plastic pumpkins and small plastic pins. Children can roll the pumpkins toward the pins, and the game can easily be adapted for children in wheelchairs.
- **Ring Toss:** A simple ring toss game using glow-in-the-dark rings or Halloween-themed

props is easy to set up and can be played by children of all abilities.

- **Arts and Crafts:** Provide a variety of Halloween-themed craft activities that can be done while sitting. Craft stations allow children to create their own decorations, masks, or spooky drawings at their own pace.

3.2 Sensory-Friendly Activities

Halloween activities can be fun without being overwhelming for kids who may have sensory processing issues. Incorporating sensory-friendly options allows more children to feel comfortable and enjoy the event.

- **Sensory Bins:** Create Halloween-themed sensory bins filled with items like fake spiders, soft cotton balls for "spider webs," or small pumpkins. Children can explore the textures and shapes in a calming environment.
- **Storytime and Quiet Areas:** Designate a quiet area where children can take a break from the action. Provide Halloween-themed storybooks or calming activities like coloring to help them relax before rejoining the fun.
- **Calm Corners:** For children who become overstimulated, having a "calm corner" with

dimmed lights, noise-canceling headphones, and soft seating can make all the difference.

3.3 Allergy-Friendly Parties

When hosting a Halloween party, it's important to consider children with food allergies or dietary restrictions. An inclusive party menu ensures that all children can enjoy the treats and snacks without worry.

- **Label Foods Clearly:** When serving food, clearly label any potential allergens, such as nuts, dairy, or gluten. Consider providing allergen-free alternatives so that no child feels left out.
- **Offer Non-Food Treats:** In addition to candy, offer non-food treats like small toys, stickers, or Halloween-themed trinkets. These can be enjoyed by all children, regardless of dietary needs.

4. Inclusive Halloween Decorations

Decorating for Halloween is one of the highlights of the season, but it's important to keep in mind that some decorations can cause anxiety or distress for certain individuals. Flashing lights, loud sounds, or hyper-realistic decorations can be particularly overwhelming for children with sensory sensitivities or anxiety.

4.1 Sensory-Friendly Decor

Opt for decorations that are visually interesting but not overwhelming. Instead of using strobe lights or jump scares, try incorporating soft lighting, glow-in-the-dark elements, or whimsical decorations like friendly ghosts or smiling pumpkins.

4.2 Avoiding Triggers

Consider the types of decorations you use and their potential impact on children with various needs. For example, avoid decorations that could be considered gory or too realistic for younger children or those with anxiety. Decorations that evoke fear can be distressing for some, so opt for a mix of spooky and fun elements.

5. Cultural Sensitivity During Halloween

While Halloween is a fun and creative holiday, it's essential to approach costume choices with cultural sensitivity in mind. Avoid costumes that perpetuate stereotypes or mock certain cultures, as this can alienate or offend individuals from different backgrounds. Celebrating Halloween inclusively also means respecting cultural differences and ensuring that all children feel valued and respected.

5.1 Avoiding Cultural Appropriation

Costumes that depict cultural or religious attire (such as Native American headdresses, traditional clothing, or sacred symbols) should be avoided, as they can be seen as disrespectful or offensive. Instead, encourage kids to choose costumes that celebrate fictional characters, animals, or professions in a way that respects all cultures.

5.2 Celebrating Diversity

Halloween can also be an opportunity to celebrate diversity and teach children about different cultures in a respectful way. Incorporate cultural traditions from around the world into your Halloween decorations or events to create a more inclusive atmosphere.

Celebrating Halloween with inclusivity and accessibility in mind ensures that no child is left out of the festivities. By making small adjustments—whether it's offering non-food treats, creating sensory-friendly spaces, or ensuring physical accessibility—you can help create a Halloween that is fun, safe, and welcoming for all.

Inclusivity fosters a sense of belonging and community spirit, which is the true magic of the holiday.

With a little extra planning and awareness, you can make Halloween a holiday where every child and family feels included, respected, and excited to participate. After all, the joy of Halloween comes from celebrating together—no matter our differences.

9.2 Sensory-Friendly Halloween for Kids with Special Needs

Halloween is a time of joy, imagination, and excitement for many children, but for kids with special needs, particularly those with sensory sensitivities, the holiday can be overwhelming. The loud noises, flashing lights, large crowds, and unexpected surprises often associated with Halloween activities can create sensory overload and anxiety. To ensure that all children, including those with special needs, can fully participate and enjoy the holiday, it's important to consider how to create a sensory-friendly Halloween environment.

This subchapter will provide a detailed guide for parents, caregivers, and event organizers to adapt Halloween traditions in ways that prioritize the needs of children with sensory processing challenges. From quiet, safe spaces to alternative activities, creating an inclusive and sensory-friendly Halloween can make the holiday more enjoyable for everyone.

1. Understanding Sensory Sensitivities and Special Needs

Sensory processing disorder (SPD) affects how individuals perceive and respond to stimuli in their environment. For children with SPD, or conditions such as autism, ADHD, or anxiety disorders, Halloween activities can present unique challenges. Bright lights, unexpected noises, crowds of people, and changes in routine can lead to sensory overload, resulting in feelings of discomfort, fear, or frustration.

1.1 What Is Sensory Processing Disorder?

Sensory processing disorder occurs when the brain has difficulty interpreting and responding appropriately to sensory information. Children with SPD may be hypersensitive (over-responsive) or hyposensitive (under-responsive) to various stimuli, such as sounds, lights, textures, or smells. This makes everyday activities, including Halloween celebrations, more stressful.

For example:

- **Hypersensitivity:** A child who is hypersensitive may feel overwhelmed by the texture of costumes, loud sounds from Halloween decorations, or the chaotic environment of a trick-or-treating event.
- **Hyposensitivity:** A child who is hyposensitive may crave more sensory input, seeking out activities that provide deep pressure, strong smells, or intense visual experiences.

Recognizing and understanding these sensory needs is the first step in creating a Halloween experience that is accessible and enjoyable for children with special needs.

2. Planning a Sensory-Friendly Halloween at Home

One of the best ways to ensure a sensory-friendly Halloween experience for children with special needs is to create a safe and comfortable environment at home. By adapting traditional Halloween activities and decorations to meet sensory needs, parents can foster a positive and enjoyable atmosphere for their children.

2.1 Choosing Costumes with Care

For many children, picking out a Halloween costume is one of the most exciting parts of the holiday. However, for kids with sensory sensitivities, wearing a costume can be uncomfortable due to certain textures, tightness, or materials. Here are some tips for selecting sensory-friendly costumes:

- **Soft and Comfortable Materials:** Choose costumes made from soft, breathable fabrics like cotton or jersey that won't irritate the skin. Avoid materials like scratchy tulle, sequins, or stiff fabrics that may cause discomfort.
- **Avoid Tight Fitting or Restrictive Outfits:** Make sure the costume is loose-fitting and allows for easy movement. Children with tactile sensitivities may become distressed if their costume feels too tight or restrictive.
- **Simple Accessories:** Some children may be sensitive to wearing hats, masks, or face paint. Instead, opt for simple accessories like headbands, lightweight capes, or handheld props that won't irritate their skin or senses.
- **Familiarize in Advance:** Allow your child to try on their costume well before Halloween night. This gives them time to get used to the feeling of the outfit and reduces the likelihood of sensory overload.

2.2 Sensory-Friendly Decorations

Halloween decorations play a big role in setting the spooky atmosphere, but some decorations may be too intense for children with special needs. When decorating your home, consider sensory-friendly alternatives that create a festive yet calming environment.

- **Soft Lighting:** Instead of using strobe lights or flashing decorations, opt for soft, warm lighting, such as fairy lights or battery-operated candles. Glow-in-the-dark elements can also add a fun, sensory-friendly touch without overwhelming the child.
- **Avoid Loud Sounds:** Skip decorations that emit loud, unexpected noises like screams, creaking doors, or howling winds. These can be startling and anxiety-inducing for kids with sensory sensitivities. Instead, choose gentle background music or no sound at all.
- **Non-Scary Decorations:** For children who may be easily frightened, avoid overly realistic or gory decorations. Stick to fun, non-scary themes like smiling pumpkins, friendly ghosts, or cartoon-style monsters.

2.3 Creating a Sensory-Safe Zone

During Halloween festivities, it's important to create a designated "safe zone" where children can retreat if they feel overwhelmed. This space should be quiet, free from loud noises, and have calming elements to help the child regulate their emotions.

- **Comfortable Seating:** Include soft seating options like bean bags, pillows, or blankets where the child can sit or lie down to decompress.
- **Calming Tools:** Provide sensory tools like fidget toys, stress balls, noise-canceling headphones, or weighted blankets to help the child self-soothe.
- **Dim Lighting:** Keep the area well-lit but not too bright. Use lamps or dimmed overhead lighting to create a calming atmosphere.
- **Quiet Time:** If your child is feeling overstimulated, allow them to take a break in the safe zone for as long as they need before returning to the festivities.

3. Sensory-Friendly Trick-or-Treating Tips

Trick-or-treating is a beloved Halloween tradition, but it can also be one of the most overwhelming activities for children with sensory sensitivities. From large crowds to noisy streets and flashing decorations, the typical trick-or-treating experience can be filled with triggers. However, with a bit of planning and flexibility, you can create a sensory-friendly trick-or-treating experience that allows your child to participate comfortably.

3.1 Pre-Plan the Route

Before heading out to trick-or-treat, plan a route that takes into consideration your child's needs. Choose quieter, less crowded neighborhoods or streets where your child can trick-or-treat without the overwhelming noise or chaos of larger groups.

- **Shorter Distances:** Consider trick-or-treating in a smaller, more contained area so your child doesn't feel pressured to walk long distances. You can even drive from house to house if needed.
- **Familiar Locations:** Stick to houses or neighborhoods that your child is familiar with to reduce anxiety about unfamiliar environments. If possible, visit homes of friends or family who understand your child's needs.
- **Set Expectations:** Talk to your child ahead of time about what to expect while trick-or-treating. Role-play common interactions like saying "trick or treat" or receiving candy to help them feel more prepared.

3.2 Alternatives to Traditional Trick-or-Treating

If traditional trick-or-treating feels too overwhelming, there are plenty of alternative ways for children to enjoy collecting treats in a more sensory-friendly environment.

- **Trunk-or-Treat:** Trunk-or-treat events are often quieter and more contained than traditional trick-or-treating. In a trunk-or-treat, families decorate their cars and park in a designated area, allowing children to collect treats in a smaller, safer space.

- **At-Home Trick-or-Treating:** For children who are more comfortable at home, you can organize a mini trick-or-treat event indoors. Set up different rooms or stations in your house where children can collect treats from family members.

- **Teal Pumpkin Project:** If your child has food allergies, consider participating in the Teal Pumpkin Project, which offers non-food treats for children who can't eat traditional Halloween candy. This inclusive initiative helps make trick-or-treating safer for children with dietary restrictions while still keeping the spirit of the holiday alive.

4. Hosting a Sensory-Friendly Halloween Party

If trick-or-treating feels too chaotic, consider hosting a sensory-friendly Halloween party at home or in your community. A controlled environment allows you to create a Halloween experience that's tailored to your child's needs, with activities that are fun and engaging without being overwhelming.

4.1 Sensory-Friendly Games

Traditional Halloween games can be modified to suit children with sensory sensitivities. Focus on games that allow children to participate at their own pace and provide a calm, supportive environment.

- **Pumpkin Painting:** Instead of carving pumpkins, which can be messy and require fine motor skills, set up a pumpkin painting station with non-toxic paints. Children can decorate their pumpkins with paint, stickers, or markers, allowing for creative expression without the sensory challenges of carving.
- **Ghost Bowling:** Use soft foam or plastic bowling pins and a lightweight ball for a fun, quiet bowling game. You can decorate the pins with ghost faces to give it a Halloween twist.
- **Sensory Bins:** Create Halloween-themed sensory bins filled with items like dried corn kernels, fake spiders, or squishy Halloween toys. Sensory bins provide a calming, tactile experience that many children find soothing.

4.2 Quiet Corners and Break Spaces

At your party, designate quiet corners or break spaces where children can retreat if they feel overstimulated. These spaces should be equipped with calming items such as noise-canceling headphones, dim lighting, and soft seating. Encourage children to take breaks whenever they need to, and make it clear that it's okay to step away from the festivities to relax.

5. Sensory-Friendly Halloween in Schools and Communities

Schools and community organizations play a big role in organizing Halloween celebrations. To ensure that all children, including those with special needs, can participate, it's important to advocate for sensory-friendly adaptations in these settings.

5.1 Modifying School Events

Schools often host Halloween parades, parties, and other events, but these activities can be overwhelming for children with sensory sensitivities. Encourage schools to offer alternatives, such as:

- **Quiet Rooms:** Provide quiet rooms or sensory-safe zones where children can go if they feel overwhelmed during school Halloween activities.
- **Costume-Free Options:** Allow children who may not be comfortable wearing costumes the

option to participate in other ways, such as
decorating or creating Halloween-themed crafts.

- **Shorter Events:** For children who find it
difficult to stay in noisy, crowded environments
for long periods of time, consider offering shorter
Halloween events with plenty of breaks.

5.2 Community Events

Community events like pumpkin patches, haunted
houses, and trunk-or-treats can also be adapted to meet
the needs of children with sensory sensitivities.

- **Sensory-Friendly Time Slots:** Some
communities offer sensory-friendly time slots
during popular Halloween events. These times
are quieter, with fewer crowds, dimmed lighting,
and reduced noise levels.
- **Inclusive Activities:** Ensure that community
Halloween events include activities that are
accessible to all children, regardless of their
sensory needs. This might include quiet craft
stations, sensory bins, or low-stimulation games.

Creating a sensory-friendly Halloween for children with
special needs allows them to enjoy the holiday in a way
that's comfortable, safe, and fun. By making small
adjustments to traditional activities—whether it's
choosing the right costume, creating quiet spaces, or

offering alternative trick-or-treating options—you can ensure that Halloween is an inclusive celebration for every child.

Halloween should be a time of joy, imagination, and community for everyone, and with a little extra planning, children with sensory sensitivities can fully participate in the excitement of the season. After all, the true spirit of Halloween is about creating memories, sharing in the fun, and making every child feel included and valued.

9.3 Halloween in Schools and Workplaces: Making It Fun for Everyone

Halloween is a time of year when people come together to celebrate creativity, imagination, and a bit of spookiness. Traditionally focused on children, this festive holiday has expanded into schools, workplaces, and community events, providing opportunities for fun and connection across age groups. However, the challenge lies in making Halloween inclusive, welcoming, and enjoyable for all. With individuals from diverse cultural backgrounds, varying comfort levels with Halloween themes, and differing needs in schools and workplaces, it's important to ensure that everyone can participate in ways that make them feel comfortable and included.

This subchapter explores how schools and workplaces can celebrate Halloween in ways that prioritize inclusivity, creativity, and accessibility, so that every person, regardless of age, background, or ability, can enjoy the festivities.

1. Creating an Inclusive Halloween in Schools

Schools are one of the primary places where Halloween is celebrated, with students eagerly anticipating costume parades, classroom parties, and fun activities. However, not all students feel comfortable participating in traditional Halloween celebrations, whether due to cultural reasons, religious beliefs, sensory sensitivities, or other factors. Inclusivity in schools means creating a space where every student can take part in the fun, without feeling left out or excluded.

1.1 Acknowledging Cultural and Religious Differences

While Halloween is a widely celebrated holiday in many countries, it is not universally observed. For some families, Halloween may conflict with their cultural or religious beliefs, and participation in traditional activities may be discouraged or even prohibited. Schools should be mindful of these differences and ensure that students who do not celebrate Halloween are not made to feel isolated or pressured.

- **Alternative Activities:** One approach to inclusivity is offering alternative, non-Halloween-themed activities for students who do not wish to participate in the holiday. This could include fall-themed activities like pumpkin decorating, harvest crafts, or nature-based projects that allow all students to engage in seasonal fun without referencing Halloween.
- **Opt-Out Options:** Schools should also allow families to opt-out of Halloween celebrations without stigma. For instance, schools can provide quiet spaces or alternative educational activities for students whose families do not observe the holiday.
- **Respectful Communication:** Open communication with parents and guardians is essential. Schools should provide clear information about planned Halloween activities and offer families the option to opt their children in or out. Additionally, schools can seek input from families on how to make celebrations more inclusive for all.

1.2 Sensory-Friendly Celebrations for Students with Special Needs

For students with sensory sensitivities or special needs, traditional Halloween celebrations can be overwhelming.

The loud noises, bright lights, unfamiliar costumes, and chaotic environment of a Halloween party can lead to sensory overload. To create a more inclusive experience, schools should consider sensory-friendly alternatives that allow all students to participate comfortably.

- **Calm, Quiet Spaces:** Provide sensory-friendly rooms or quiet areas where students can take breaks if they become overwhelmed by the sensory input of Halloween activities. These spaces should include dim lighting, soft seating, and calming items like noise-canceling headphones, sensory toys, or fidget tools.
- **Adapted Costumes:** Encourage students to wear costumes that are comfortable and sensory-friendly. For example, costumes made from soft fabrics and without restrictive accessories can make the experience more enjoyable for students with tactile sensitivities.
- **Controlled Environment:** Instead of loud, chaotic Halloween parties, schools can host quieter, more structured activities, such as craft stations, pumpkin decorating, or storytelling sessions. These activities can be designed to engage students in a fun, calm, and supportive environment.

1.3 Encouraging Participation Without Pressure

Some students may feel uncomfortable dressing up or participating in Halloween activities for personal or social reasons. Inclusivity in schools means respecting these feelings and providing a range of ways for students to join in the fun without pressure.

- **Costume-Free Options:** Not all students may want to wear costumes. Schools can offer alternative ways for students to express their creativity, such as wearing themed colors (like orange and black) or participating in non-costume activities like decorating pumpkins, making Halloween crafts, or engaging in themed games.
- **Group Activities:** Encourage collaborative activities that allow students to work together, regardless of whether they are in costume. For example, a class project where students create a Halloween-themed mural or a group storytelling activity can promote inclusion and team spirit without focusing on costumes.
- **Positive Reinforcement:** Teachers and staff should promote an environment where all forms of participation are celebrated, whether a student is fully dressed in costume, wearing a simple accessory, or choosing not to dress up at all. This helps reduce social pressure and ensures that

students feel comfortable engaging at their own level.

2. Celebrating Halloween in Workplaces

In many workplaces, Halloween has become a popular event, with employees dressing up in costumes, decorating their offices, and participating in themed parties or contests. However, just as in schools, workplaces need to be mindful of creating an inclusive and respectful environment during Halloween celebrations. Employees come from diverse backgrounds, and not everyone may feel comfortable with the themes associated with Halloween, such as ghosts, witches, or horror elements. Additionally, some employees may have physical or sensory needs that should be considered in the planning of Halloween events.

2.1 Respecting Diverse Beliefs and Preferences

Not all employees celebrate Halloween, and for some, the themes associated with the holiday may conflict with their personal, religious, or cultural beliefs. It's important for workplaces to acknowledge and respect these differences, while still providing opportunities for those who do wish to participate.

- **Optional Participation:** Halloween events in the workplace should always be optional. Employees should never feel pressured to participate in costume contests, parties, or other themed activities. Managers should make it clear that opting out of Halloween celebrations will not impact an employee's standing or relationships within the workplace.
- **Neutral Themes:** To foster inclusivity, workplaces can consider focusing on neutral, fall-themed events instead of explicitly Halloween-themed activities. For example, hosting a "Harvest Festival" or "Autumn Celebration" allows employees to enjoy seasonal fun without referencing potentially sensitive Halloween themes.
- **Open Dialogue:** Managers and event organizers should encourage open dialogue about Halloween celebrations, allowing employees to express their preferences and concerns. By seeking input from employees, workplaces can create a celebration that reflects the diverse values and interests of the team.

2.2 Inclusive Costumes and Dress Code Policies

Workplace costume contests and dress-up events are a fun way for employees to express their creativity, but they also come with challenges. Some costumes may unintentionally offend or exclude others, while others may not be appropriate for a professional environment. To ensure that costume celebrations are fun and inclusive, workplaces should provide clear guidelines and encourage respectful participation.

- **Costume Guidelines:** Workplaces should establish costume guidelines that promote inclusivity and professionalism. Costumes that are culturally insensitive, offensive, or overly revealing should be discouraged. Additionally, workplaces can encourage employees to avoid costumes that involve fake weapons or violent themes, as these may be inappropriate for a professional setting.
- **Costume Alternatives:** For employees who may not feel comfortable dressing up, workplaces can offer alternative ways to participate, such as themed accessories (like Halloween pins or scarves) or a casual dress code that reflects the season.
- **Inclusive Themes:** To ensure that everyone feels welcome to participate, workplaces can suggest costume themes that are broad and inclusive. For example, a "superheroes" or "favorite movie characters" theme allows employees to choose costumes that reflect their personal interests without being tied to specific Halloween themes.

2.3 Sensory-Friendly Considerations in the Workplace

Just as in schools, employees in the workplace may have sensory sensitivities that make traditional Halloween celebrations overwhelming. Loud music, flashing lights, and crowded events can create discomfort for some employees. To create a more inclusive environment, workplaces should consider sensory-friendly options.

- **Quiet Zones:** During Halloween events, provide quiet areas where employees can take breaks from the festivities if they need a sensory reprieve. These areas should be free from loud music, bright lights, and strong smells, offering a calming space for employees to relax.
- **Sensory-Friendly Decorations:** Avoid overly stimulating decorations like strobe lights, loud sound effects, or decorations that emit strong smells. Instead, opt for softer lighting, calming colors, and simple, non-intrusive decorations that create a festive atmosphere without overwhelming the senses.
- **Flexible Participation:** Some employees may prefer not to attend large Halloween parties or events due to sensory sensitivities. Workplaces should offer flexible participation options, such as virtual activities, small-group events, or

non-party-based celebrations like pumpkin decorating or a themed potluck.

3. Fun, Inclusive Halloween Activities for Schools and Workplaces

Whether in schools or workplaces, the key to an inclusive Halloween celebration is offering a variety of activities that appeal to different interests and abilities. By providing a range of options, you can ensure that everyone feels welcome to participate in a way that's comfortable and enjoyable for them.

3.1 Creative Group Activities

Collaborative group activities allow individuals to participate in Halloween celebrations without feeling isolated or pressured. These activities promote teamwork, creativity, and fun, making them a great addition to school or workplace events.

- **Pumpkin Decorating Contests:** Instead of traditional carving, host a pumpkin decorating contest where participants can use paint, markers, stickers, and other materials to create their designs. This allows for more creativity and less mess, making it accessible to everyone.
- **Halloween-Themed Crafts:** Set up a craft station where participants can make their own

Halloween decorations, such as paper bats, ghost garlands, or pumpkin masks. This is a great option for individuals who may not want to wear costumes but still want to get into the Halloween spirit.

- **Storytelling Circles:** In schools, teachers can organize Halloween-themed storytelling circles where students can share their favorite spooky stories or create their own. In workplaces, employees can participate in a "story slam" where they tell funny or spooky Halloween anecdotes.

3.2 Virtual Halloween Celebrations

For schools and workplaces with remote participants, virtual Halloween celebrations can be just as fun and engaging. Hosting online activities ensures that everyone, including those working or learning from home, can participate in the festivities.

- **Virtual Costume Contests:** Host a virtual costume contest where participants can show off their costumes on camera. For those who prefer not to dress up, consider offering a "best Halloween background" contest, where participants decorate their virtual meeting backgrounds.

- **Online Halloween Games:** Organize virtual games like Halloween trivia, scavenger hunts, or "guess the Halloween movie" quizzes. These games can be tailored to suit the interests and age groups of the participants.
- **Virtual Pumpkin Decorating:** Provide participants with a virtual pumpkin template that they can decorate using online tools. Share the decorated pumpkins during a virtual event and vote on the most creative designs.

By taking the time to plan inclusive, accessible, and respectful Halloween celebrations in schools and workplaces, we create an environment where everyone can share in the joy and creativity of the holiday. Whether through offering alternative activities, adapting to sensory needs, or providing flexible participation options, schools and workplaces can ensure that Halloween is a time of fun, connection, and celebration for all.

Ultimately, an inclusive Halloween is one that embraces diversity, encourages creativity, and makes everyone feel welcome—whether they're donning a spooky costume or simply enjoying the festive atmosphere.

CHAPTER 10: HALLOWEEN MARKETING AND POP CULTURE

10.1 Halloween on Screen: Iconic Movies and TV Shows

Halloween is not only a beloved holiday celebrated through costumes, trick-or-treating, and spooky decorations; it is also a significant part of popular culture, especially on screen. From iconic horror films to family-friendly Halloween specials, movies and TV shows have played a huge role in shaping the public's perception of the holiday. This section will dive into the most influential Halloween-themed films and TV shows that have become synonymous with the holiday, exploring how these productions have contributed to the broader cultural imagination surrounding Halloween.

1.1 Horror Classics: The Birth of Halloween on Screen

Halloween has long been associated with the horror genre, and some of the most iconic horror films of all time take place during this spooky season. These movies not only define the genre but also have become a cultural cornerstone for Halloween celebrations, influencing costume choices, decorations, and haunted house themes.

- **John Carpenter's *Halloween* (1978):** Perhaps the most famous Halloween-themed movie of all time, *Halloween* is a slasher film that introduced audiences to Michael Myers, the masked serial killer who haunts the fictional town of Haddonfield. The film's chilling theme music and the character of Michael Myers have since become symbols of Halloween horror. The success of *Halloween* launched a franchise with multiple sequels, prequels, and reboots, reinforcing its place as a Halloween staple.
- ***A Nightmare on Elm Street* (1984):** Another horror classic that often finds its way into Halloween movie marathons is *A Nightmare on Elm Street*. The film introduces Freddy Krueger, a villain who haunts the dreams of teenagers. While not directly set on Halloween, the film's frightening tone, supernatural elements, and dark

visuals make it a perfect fit for Halloween viewing.

- ***Hocus Pocus* (1993):** For those who prefer a lighter, more family-friendly approach to Halloween, *Hocus Pocus* has become an essential part of the holiday season. The film tells the story of three witches, the Sanderson sisters, who are resurrected on Halloween night. With its blend of humor, magic, and nostalgia, *Hocus Pocus* has developed a cult following and is frequently re-aired on TV during the Halloween season.

1.2 Halloween-Themed TV Shows: Spooky Episodes and Specials

Television has also embraced Halloween, with many TV shows airing special episodes or holiday-themed events that capture the spooky spirit of the season. These episodes not only entertain but often provide a sense of nostalgia for viewers who associate them with their own Halloween memories.

- ***The Simpsons: Treehouse of Horror* Specials:** The *Treehouse of Horror* series has become an annual tradition for fans of *The Simpsons*. Airing every Halloween since 1990, these episodes parody famous horror films, literature, and TV shows while incorporating the quirky humor of *The Simpsons*. With over 30 installments,

Treehouse of Horror has become a defining element of Halloween on TV, offering both laughs and spooky fun.

- ***Buffy the Vampire Slayer* Halloween Episodes:** As a show already set in a world filled with vampires, demons, and magic, *Buffy the Vampire Slayer* naturally lent itself to Halloween themes. The series featured several Halloween-themed episodes, with the characters often facing supernatural threats specific to the holiday. These episodes remain fan favorites, blending horror, humor, and heartfelt moments.

- ***Stranger Things* (2016):** Although not explicitly a Halloween series, *Stranger Things* incorporates many elements of 1980s horror and sci-fi, making it a perfect fit for Halloween viewing. Set in the small town of Hawkins, Indiana, the show features a group of kids battling supernatural creatures from the "Upside Down" while paying homage to classic horror films. Its Halloween episodes, particularly in Season 2, where the characters dress up as Ghostbusters, have contributed to its status as a Halloween favorite.

1.3 How Movies and TV Shape Halloween Culture

Movies and TV shows are powerful tools in shaping how Halloween is celebrated, not only by providing entertainment but by influencing the aesthetics and traditions associated with the holiday. Iconic characters like Michael Myers, Freddy Krueger, and the Sanderson sisters have inspired countless Halloween costumes, while the visuals of haunted houses, pumpkins, and ghosts from these films and shows have become central to Halloween décor.

Moreover, the tradition of Halloween movie marathons—where people gather to watch their favorite horror films or TV specials—has become an integral part of how many people celebrate the holiday. Whether enjoying the thrill of a slasher film or the nostalgia of a childhood favorite, Halloween on screen plays a key role in how the holiday is experienced across generations.

10.2 The Business of Halloween: From Candy to Costumes

Halloween is not only a cultural event but also a major economic force. In fact, Halloween has grown to become one of the most profitable holidays in the world, with businesses capitalizing on the demand for costumes, candy, decorations, and more. From retail to marketing, Halloween has evolved into a commercial phenomenon that generates billions of dollars annually.

2.1 The Rise of Halloween Spending

Over the past few decades, Halloween spending has skyrocketed. What was once a modest holiday focused on children trick-or-treating has transformed into a multi-billion-dollar industry that appeals to people of all ages. According to the National Retail Federation (NRF), Americans alone spend more than $10 billion on Halloween each year, with that figure continuing to grow. The key areas of spending include costumes, candy, decorations, and parties.

- **Costumes:** Costumes are a major part of Halloween spending, with millions of people, including adults, purchasing or creating outfits each year. Popular costumes are often influenced by the latest trends in pop culture, from movie characters to viral internet sensations. Retailers capitalize on these trends by offering a wide range of costume options, from pre-made costumes to DIY kits that allow people to create their own looks.
- **Candy:** Candy is another significant part of Halloween spending. In the United States, Halloween is the largest candy-purchasing holiday, with companies producing special themed candies, packaging, and flavors specifically for the occasion. Popular brands such as Reese's, M&M's, and Snickers produce

limited-edition products to align with Halloween, boosting their sales during this time.

- **Decorations:** Halloween has also seen a boom in decorations, as more and more people decorate their homes for the holiday. From inflatable lawn decorations to intricate haunted house setups, Halloween has become a time for people to showcase their creativity and transform their homes into spooky spectacles.

2.2 The Growth of Adult Participation in Halloween

One of the key drivers of Halloween's commercial success is the increased participation of adults in the holiday. In the past, Halloween was primarily seen as a children's holiday, focused on trick-or-treating and school parties. However, in recent years, more adults have embraced the holiday, hosting themed parties, dressing up in elaborate costumes, and decorating their homes.

This shift has expanded the market for Halloween products, with retailers offering a wider range of costumes, decorations, and party supplies aimed at adults. Halloween parties for adults often feature themed cocktails, elaborate décor, and costume contests, creating demand for higher-end, more sophisticated products that go beyond traditional children's items.

- **Haunted Attractions:** Another area where Halloween has grown is in haunted attractions. Haunted houses, corn mazes, and hayrides have become popular forms of entertainment for adults and families during the Halloween season. These attractions range from small local events to large-scale, professional productions that draw crowds from across the country. Haunted attractions have become a significant part of the Halloween economy, generating revenue through ticket sales and merchandise.

- **Pet Costumes:** An unexpected but rapidly growing segment of Halloween spending is pet costumes. With more people viewing their pets as members of the family, pet costumes have become a popular way to include furry friends in the Halloween festivities. Retailers have responded to this trend by offering a wide variety of pet costumes, from simple pumpkin outfits to elaborate superhero ensembles.

2.3 Halloween and Brand Marketing

For businesses, Halloween presents a unique opportunity for marketing and brand engagement. Companies use Halloween as a platform for creative advertising campaigns, themed products, and limited-time promotions. From food and beverage companies to clothing brands, businesses across industries leverage Halloween to increase sales and create memorable marketing experiences.

- **Limited-Edition Products:** Many companies release limited-edition products during the Halloween season, from Halloween-themed packaging to new seasonal flavors. For example, Starbucks' Pumpkin Spice Latte has become synonymous with the fall season, while candy companies release special-edition Halloween treats.
- **Halloween-Themed Advertising Campaigns:** Halloween provides a chance for brands to get creative with their advertising. From spooky commercials to social media challenges, companies use Halloween as a way to engage with consumers in fun and unexpected ways. Brands often collaborate with influencers or celebrities to create viral Halloween campaigns that generate buzz on social media.
- **Interactive Experiences:** Some brands take Halloween marketing a step further by creating interactive experiences for consumers. For example, escape rooms, haunted mazes, and virtual reality experiences have become popular ways for companies to immerse consumers in Halloween-themed environments. These

experiences not only drive sales but also foster brand loyalty by offering unique and memorable interactions with the brand.

10.3 Social Media and Halloween Trends: How Influencers Shape the Holiday

In the digital age, social media has become a driving force in shaping trends and influencing how holidays like Halloween are celebrated. Platforms like Instagram, TikTok, and Pinterest are filled with Halloween-themed content, from DIY costume tutorials to spooky makeup looks, and influencers play a significant role in shaping how people engage with the holiday.

3.1 Instagram and the Rise of Visual Halloween Content

Instagram, with its focus on visuals, has become a hub for Halloween inspiration. Influencers and everyday users alike share their Halloween experiences through pictures and videos, showcasing costumes, decorations, and party setups. Hashtags like #Halloween, #SpookySeason, and #HalloweenCostume dominate the platform during October, offering endless inspiration for those looking to create the perfect Halloween look or theme.

- **DIY Costume Tutorials:** Instagram is filled with DIY costume tutorials, where influencers and creators share step-by-step guides on how to make creative, affordable costumes at home. These tutorials often go viral, influencing what costumes people choose to wear and how they approach their Halloween outfits.
- **Halloween Makeup Looks:** Makeup influencers have also played a significant role in shaping Halloween trends. Spooky or glamorous Halloween makeup looks are often shared on Instagram, with influencers offering tips on how to achieve dramatic effects using makeup. From skeleton face paint to elaborate witch looks, these makeup tutorials have become an essential part of the Halloween preparation process for many.
- **Home Décor Inspiration:** Influencers specializing in home décor also play a role in shaping Halloween trends. Many share photos of their elaborately decorated homes, providing followers with ideas for how to transform their own spaces into spooky havens. From gothic-inspired themes to cute and whimsical setups, home décor influencers drive trends in Halloween decorating.

3.2 TikTok and Viral Halloween Challenges

TikTok has emerged as a platform where Halloween trends spread like wildfire. From dance challenges to costume reveals, TikTok creators use short videos to share their Halloween ideas, often setting the stage for viral trends that are quickly adopted by users worldwide.

- **Costume Reveal Challenges:** On TikTok, one popular trend is the costume reveal challenge, where users create videos showing off their Halloween costumes in a fun and dramatic way. These videos often involve a transition from everyday clothing to full costume, accompanied by music or special effects. This trend has encouraged creativity and participation, with users showcasing everything from simple DIY costumes to elaborate, professionally made outfits.
- **Spooky Dance Challenges:** Another major Halloween trend on TikTok is the spooky dance challenge, where users create choreography to popular Halloween-themed songs, such as *Thriller* or *Ghostbusters*. These challenges are often accompanied by costumes or makeup looks, adding to the fun and engaging nature of the content. The viral nature of these dance

challenges allows users to connect and participate in Halloween celebrations, even if they're not attending physical events.

- **Halloween Storytelling:** Storytelling is also a popular Halloween activity on TikTok. Creators use the platform to share spooky stories, often in a series of short videos. Some creators specialize in telling ghost stories or urban legends, while others share personal experiences with the supernatural. This trend not only entertains but also adds a layer of mystery and excitement to the Halloween season.

3.3 Pinterest and the Planning of Halloween Celebrations

Pinterest has long been a go-to platform for holiday planning, and Halloween is no exception. From costume ideas to party themes, Pinterest offers a treasure trove of Halloween inspiration for those looking to create the perfect spooky celebration.

- **Halloween Party Planning:** Pinterest users often create boards dedicated to Halloween party planning, pinning ideas for decorations, food, and activities. These boards offer a one-stop shop for anyone looking to host a Halloween party, with detailed suggestions for everything from invitations to spooky cocktails.

- **DIY Projects:** Pinterest is also a popular platform for DIY Halloween projects. Users share tutorials and ideas for homemade costumes, decorations, and treats. These DIY projects not only provide inspiration but also encourage creativity and resourcefulness, making Halloween accessible to those on a budget.
- **Halloween Recipes:** Halloween-themed food and drink ideas are also widely shared on Pinterest. From spooky snacks like "mummy hot dogs" to creative desserts like "ghost cupcakes," Pinterest is a go-to resource for those looking to add a fun and festive touch to their Halloween meals.

3.4 How Influencers Shape Halloween Trends

Influencers have become key players in shaping Halloween trends, offering their followers a mix of inspiration, tutorials, and product recommendations. From fashion influencers showcasing the latest Halloween costumes to makeup artists offering spooky beauty looks, influencers provide their audiences with the tools and ideas needed to fully embrace the holiday.

- **Sponsored Content:** Many influencers collaborate with brands to promote Halloween products, from costumes and makeup to decorations and candy. These collaborations often include discount codes or giveaways, encouraging followers to purchase the products featured in the influencers' posts. By working with influencers, brands can reach a larger audience and increase their sales during the Halloween season.

- **Collaborative Events:** Some influencers even host their own Halloween events, both online and in-person. These events often include costume contests, makeup tutorials, or live storytelling sessions, allowing followers to engage directly with the influencer and participate in Halloween activities in a fun and interactive way.

Halloween has transformed from a simple, spooky celebration into a major cultural and economic event, driven in large part by the influence of movies, TV shows, and social media trends. From iconic horror films to viral TikTok challenges, pop culture and marketing have shaped how Halloween is celebrated, making it a holiday that transcends generations and appeals to people of all ages.

The business of Halloween has also expanded dramatically, with brands leveraging the holiday for creative marketing campaigns, product launches, and themed experiences. As influencers continue to play a key role in shaping Halloween trends, the holiday will likely continue to evolve, offering new ways for people to engage with the spooky season both online and offline.

Ultimately, whether you're watching a classic Halloween movie, dressing up in a DIY costume, or participating in a viral social media challenge, Halloween has become a cultural phenomenon that goes far beyond its origins, blending entertainment, commerce, and creativity into one of the most beloved holidays of the year.

CHAPTER 11: THE FUTURE OF HALLOWEEN

As one of the most beloved and evolving holidays, Halloween continues to change with the times. In the past few decades, we've seen it grow from a simple celebration of spooky fun to a massive commercial and cultural event. However, like any tradition, it must adapt to new challenges and opportunities. In this chapter, we'll explore three significant areas where Halloween is evolving: sustainability, technology, and the aftermath of the global pandemic.

11.1 Sustainable Halloween: Reducing Waste Without Sacrificing Fun

With growing awareness of environmental issues, more people are looking for ways to celebrate Halloween in a sustainable manner without losing the fun and excitement that makes the holiday special. Sustainability has become an important part of many conversations, and Halloween is no exception. From eco-friendly costumes to reducing candy wrapper waste, people are discovering new ways to enjoy the festivities while being mindful of their environmental footprint.

The Environmental Impact of Halloween

Halloween, while a time for fun and creativity, can also generate significant waste. According to research, millions of pounds of costumes, decorations, and candy wrappers end up in landfills after the holiday each year. Many of these items are made from non-recyclable materials, contributing to pollution and waste.

- **Costumes:** Many store-bought costumes are made from synthetic materials like polyester, which is not biodegradable and contributes to plastic pollution. After a single use, these costumes often get discarded, contributing to the growing waste problem.
- **Decorations:** Halloween decorations, particularly plastic pumpkins, fake cobwebs, and other synthetic items, are also major contributors to waste. Most of these decorations are not designed for long-term use and end up in the trash after a few seasons.
- **Candy Wrappers:** While candy is a staple of Halloween, the individually wrapped treats result in enormous amounts of plastic waste. Traditional candy wrappers are not recyclable,

which means they add to the holiday's overall environmental footprint.

Despite these challenges, there are many ways to make Halloween more sustainable without sacrificing the fun and excitement of the season.

Eco-Friendly Costumes: Creativity Meets Sustainability

One of the best ways to celebrate a sustainable Halloween is by making eco-friendly costume choices. Instead of purchasing new costumes made from synthetic materials, consider these alternatives:

- **DIY Costumes:** Creating your own costume from materials you already have is a fun and environmentally friendly option. You can repurpose old clothes, household items, or fabric scraps to create a unique and personalized costume. Not only does this reduce waste, but it also allows for greater creativity.
- **Second-Hand Costumes:** Thrift stores and online marketplaces like eBay and Poshmark are great places to find second-hand costumes. Buying used costumes not only reduces waste but also saves money. Additionally, you can donate or swap costumes with friends and family to give them a second life.

- **Costume Rentals:** Another sustainable option is renting costumes. Many costume rental shops offer a wide variety of options, allowing you to wear a high-quality costume without the environmental impact of purchasing a new one.
- **Sustainable Materials:** For those who prefer to buy new costumes, look for options made from sustainable materials like organic cotton or recycled fabrics. Some companies are now producing eco-friendly Halloween costumes that are both stylish and sustainable.

Eco-Conscious Decorations: Spooky Yet Sustainable

Halloween decorations are another area where sustainability can make a big difference. Instead of purchasing disposable, plastic decorations, consider these eco-friendly alternatives:

- **DIY Decorations:** Homemade decorations can be a fun and creative way to reduce waste. You can use natural materials like pumpkins, gourds, and dried leaves to create festive displays. For example, carving a pumpkin not only provides a fun activity but also results in a biodegradable decoration that can be composted after Halloween.
- **Reusable Decorations:** Invest in high-quality, reusable decorations that you can use year after

year. Instead of buying single-use items, look for durable decorations made from materials like wood, metal, or fabric. You can also upcycle items from around your home to create unique Halloween displays.

- **Energy-Efficient Lighting:** If you enjoy lighting up your home for Halloween, consider using energy-efficient LED lights or solar-powered options. These lights use less energy and last longer than traditional incandescent bulbs, making them a more sustainable choice.

Sustainable Treats: Reducing Candy Waste

Candy is a central part of Halloween, but the individually wrapped treats contribute significantly to plastic waste. Here are some ways to enjoy Halloween treats while reducing your environmental impact:

- **Buy in Bulk:** Purchasing candy in bulk can help reduce the amount of packaging waste. You can then distribute the candy in reusable containers or paper bags instead of plastic wrappers.
- **Eco-Friendly Candy Brands:** Some candy brands are now offering environmentally friendly packaging options, such as compostable wrappers or recyclable materials. Supporting these brands can help reduce the overall waste generated by Halloween treats.

- **Homemade Treats:** If you're hosting a Halloween party, consider making homemade treats like cookies, cupcakes, or popcorn balls. These can be packaged in reusable or biodegradable containers, reducing the need for single-use wrappers.
- **Candy Alternatives:** Non-candy treats, like stickers, pencils, or small toys, can be a fun and sustainable alternative to traditional Halloween candy. These items can be reused or recycled, making them a more eco-friendly option.

Community Involvement: Encouraging Sustainable Halloween Practices

Promoting sustainable Halloween practices can be a community effort. Here are some ways to get your community involved in reducing Halloween waste:

- **Neighborhood Costume Swaps:** Organize a neighborhood costume swap where families can exchange gently used costumes. This not only reduces waste but also helps families save money on new costumes.
- **Eco-Friendly Events:** Host a sustainable Halloween event in your community, such as a DIY decoration workshop or a sustainable costume contest. These events can help raise

awareness about the importance of reducing waste while celebrating the holiday.

- **Trick-or-Treat Recycling Stations:** Set up recycling stations in your neighborhood where trick-or-treaters can dispose of candy wrappers in an eco-friendly way. Encourage families to bring reusable bags for collecting candy instead of using plastic bags.

By making small changes to the way we celebrate Halloween, we can significantly reduce the environmental impact of the holiday while still enjoying all the fun and excitement it has to offer.

11.2 Tech-Savvy Halloween: Virtual Reality, Digital Decorations, and More

As technology continues to advance, Halloween is becoming increasingly tech-savvy. From virtual reality haunted houses to interactive digital decorations, technology is transforming the way we celebrate this spooky holiday. In this section, we'll explore some of the most exciting tech innovations shaping the future of Halloween.

Virtual Reality (VR) and Augmented Reality (AR) Experiences

One of the most significant ways technology is changing Halloween is through virtual reality (VR) and augmented reality (AR) experiences. These immersive technologies allow users to experience Halloween in entirely new ways, blurring the line between the digital and physical worlds.

- **Virtual Haunted Houses:** VR haunted houses have become a popular attraction for those seeking a thrilling Halloween experience. Using VR headsets, participants can explore eerie, haunted environments filled with ghosts, monsters, and other spooky surprises. These virtual haunted houses offer a safe, yet immersive way to experience the fear and excitement of a traditional haunted house.
- **AR Halloween Games:** Augmented reality games, like *Pokémon GO*, have also become a popular Halloween activity. Some AR apps allow users to hunt for virtual ghosts or monsters in their real-world environment, creating a fun and interactive Halloween adventure.
- **Interactive Halloween Parties:** With the rise of virtual events, many people are now hosting virtual Halloween parties using platforms like Zoom or VRChat. These parties often feature

virtual costumes, spooky backgrounds, and interactive games, allowing participants to celebrate Halloween with friends and family from anywhere in the world.

Digital Decorations: Bringing Halloween to Life

Digital decorations are another exciting tech innovation that is transforming the way we decorate for Halloween. Instead of traditional physical decorations, digital projectors and smart lighting systems can create dynamic, interactive displays that bring Halloween scenes to life.

- **Digital Projectors:** Digital projectors are becoming a popular way to create high-tech Halloween displays. These projectors can be used to project spooky animations, such as ghosts or zombies, onto the walls of your home. Some projectors even come with preloaded Halloween scenes, allowing you to create a haunted house atmosphere with minimal effort.
- **Smart Lighting:** Smart lighting systems, like Philips Hue, allow homeowners to create custom Halloween lighting effects. These systems can be programmed to change colors, flicker, or flash in sync with Halloween music or sound effects, creating a fully immersive Halloween experience.

- **Interactive Displays:** Some companies are now offering interactive Halloween displays that respond to movement or sound. For example, motion-activated digital displays can surprise trick-or-treaters with spooky animations as they approach your front door.

Tech-Enhanced Costumes: The Future of Dressing Up

Technology is also making its way into Halloween costumes, with new innovations that take dressing up to the next level. From LED-illuminated costumes to wearable tech, these high-tech costumes are sure to impress.

- **LED Costumes:** LED lights can be incorporated into costumes to create glowing, animated effects. For example, a child dressed as a robot might have LED lights embedded in their costume that light up in sync with their movements. These tech-enhanced costumes are not only visually striking but also improve safety by making trick-or-treaters more visible in the dark.
- **Wearable Tech Costumes:** Some high-tech costumes feature wearable technology, such as motion sensors or sound effects. For example, a superhero costume might include built-in sensors

that trigger sound effects or LED lights when the wearer strikes a certain pose.

Social Media and Halloween: Staying Connected Through Technology

Social media continues to play a significant role in how people celebrate Halloween. Platforms like Instagram, TikTok, and YouTube are filled with Halloween content, from costume tutorials to spooky makeup transformations. Here's how social media is shaping Halloween:

- **Costume Challenges:** Social media platforms are often home to Halloween costume challenges, where users create and share their best costume ideas. These challenges not only inspire creativity but also bring people together to celebrate the holiday online.
- **DIY Tutorials:** YouTube and TikTok are filled with Halloween DIY tutorials, from makeup looks to costume ideas. These tutorials make it easy for anyone to create a stunning Halloween look using items they already have at home.
- **Sharing the Fun:** Many people now share their Halloween experiences on social media, from photos of their costumes to videos of their decorated homes. Social media platforms allow

people to connect and celebrate the holiday together, even if they're miles apart.

11.3 Post-Pandemic Halloween: How Global Events Have Shaped the Holiday's Future

The global COVID-19 pandemic had a profound impact on holidays and social gatherings, and Halloween was no exception. The pandemic forced people to rethink how they celebrated, and in many cases, it led to new traditions and practices. As we move into the future, the effects of the pandemic will continue to shape how Halloween is celebrated.

The Rise of Outdoor and Contactless Celebrations

One of the most significant changes to Halloween during the pandemic was the shift toward outdoor and contactless celebrations. Many traditional Halloween activities, such as indoor parties and crowded haunted houses, were no longer feasible during the height of the pandemic. In response, people found creative ways to celebrate safely.

- **Outdoor Trick-or-Treating:** To reduce the risk of transmission, many communities adapted their trick-or-treating practices. Some neighborhoods set up outdoor candy stations where trick-or-treaters could collect treats without coming into close contact with others. Others used creative solutions like candy chutes or "grab-and-go" treat bags.

- **Drive-Through Events:** Drive-through Halloween events became a popular alternative to traditional haunted houses and parties. These events allowed families to enjoy spooky displays and attractions from the safety of their vehicles. Some drive-through events even featured live actors and animatronics, creating an immersive experience.

Virtual Celebrations and the Future of Halloween

As mentioned earlier, virtual celebrations became a common way to celebrate Halloween during the pandemic. While many people are eager to return to in-person gatherings, virtual events are likely to remain a part of Halloween's future. Virtual costume contests, movie nights, and haunted house tours offer a safe and convenient way to celebrate with friends and family, especially for those who are unable to attend in-person events.

Health and Safety Considerations in the Post-Pandemic World

While the immediate threat of COVID-19 may have subsided, the pandemic has heightened awareness of health and safety considerations during holidays like Halloween. Moving forward, we may see lasting changes to how Halloween is celebrated, with a greater emphasis on hygiene and safety.

- **Hand Sanitizer Stations:** Many communities now provide hand sanitizer stations at Halloween events, and this practice is likely to continue in the future. These stations help reduce the spread of germs, especially in high-traffic areas like trick-or-treating routes.
- **Mask Wearing:** While Halloween masks have always been a part of the holiday, the pandemic introduced the idea of wearing masks for health reasons. Some people may continue to incorporate face masks into their costumes, either for safety or as a creative addition to their look.

Halloween is a holiday that thrives on creativity and adaptation, and its future is no exception. As we become more mindful of sustainability, embrace new technologies, and adapt to the post-pandemic world, Halloween will continue to evolve. Whether through eco-friendly costumes, virtual haunted houses, or contactless trick-or-treating, the future of Halloween promises to be just as thrilling and fun as ever.

CONCLUSION: THE MAGIC OF HALLOWEEN UNMASKED

Halloween is a holiday brimming with imagination, mystery, and timeless traditions that capture the hearts of people across generations. But what makes Halloween so special? It is the way the holiday invites creativity, community, and personal expression. Whether through crafting a unique costume, hosting a haunted house party, or simply trick-or-treating with loved ones, the magic of Halloween lies in the memories and traditions that we create year after year.

In this conclusion, we will explore how you can harness the magic of Halloween to create your own traditions, embrace its spirit, and celebrate in ways that are meaningful and personal to you. From small, cozy rituals to large, festive gatherings, Halloween offers endless opportunities for fun, creativity, and connection. Let's dive into the ways you can make the holiday your own and continue to cherish it for years to come.

1. How to Create Your Own Halloween Traditions

Halloween has a rich history filled with customs that have evolved over centuries, yet the beauty of this holiday is its flexibility. While there are time-honored traditions like carving pumpkins, dressing in costumes, and trick-or-treating, Halloween also gives us the freedom to invent our own rituals and celebrations. This section will guide you through the process of creating personalized traditions that reflect your unique style, interests, and values.

1.1 Embrace Your Passions: Infusing Personal Interests into Halloween

One of the best ways to create lasting Halloween traditions is by incorporating your personal passions and hobbies into the holiday. Whether you're an avid reader, a movie buff, or a crafting enthusiast, you can blend your interests with Halloween to create memorable experiences.

- **For Book Lovers:** If you love reading, consider hosting a Halloween-themed book club where everyone reads spooky or gothic novels throughout October. Share favorite passages, discuss the eerie settings, and even dress up as characters from the books.

- **For Movie Enthusiasts:** Create a Halloween movie marathon tradition, inviting friends or family over to watch classic horror films, animated Halloween specials, or even funny Halloween-themed comedies. You can elevate the experience with themed snacks like "witch's brew" punch or "mummy" hot dogs.
- **For Crafters:** If you enjoy crafting, you can turn Halloween into a season of DIY magic. Host a craft night where everyone creates their own Halloween decorations, costumes, or even homemade trick-or-treat bags. This is a great way to build memories while adding a personal touch to your holiday.

1.2 Family Traditions: Creating Spooky Memories Together

Halloween is an ideal holiday for families to come together and bond over fun, spooky activities. Whether you have young children or a large extended family, you can create traditions that will be cherished for generations.

- **Annual Pumpkin Carving Contest:** Make pumpkin carving an annual family event, with everyone participating in a contest. Each family member can design and carve their own pumpkin, and then vote on the funniest, scariest, or most creative design. This can be done over a cozy evening with hot apple cider, music, and laughter.
- **Trick-or-Treat Maps:** For families who love trick-or-treating, create a tradition where you map out the best neighborhoods or homes with the spookiest decorations. Turn it into an adventure by making a checklist of "must-visit" houses with impressive displays, and take pictures each year to document your trick-or-treating journey.
- **Spooky Storytelling Night:** Create a family tradition of gathering around the fire or candles to share spooky stories. You can retell classic ghost tales or make up your own eerie adventures. This is a great way to foster imagination, especially for young kids, while enjoying quality family time.

1.3 Hosting Annual Halloween Gatherings

For those who love to entertain, Halloween presents the perfect opportunity to host an annual gathering that friends and family will look forward to each year. You can start your own Halloween party tradition, whether it's a themed costume party, a haunted house experience, or a pumpkin-themed feast.

- **Themed Costume Parties:** A costume party is a staple of Halloween, but you can take it to the next level by creating specific themes each year. One year, you might host a "classic movie monsters" party, while the next year could be a "superheroes vs. villains" theme. This keeps your Halloween gatherings fresh and exciting, as guests will eagerly anticipate what the next theme will be.
- **DIY Haunted House:** If you love a good scare, consider turning your home into a haunted house each year. With just a few spooky decorations, eerie sound effects, and dim lighting, you can create an immersive Halloween experience for your guests. You can even add interactive elements like scavenger hunts or puzzles that lead them through the haunted areas.
- **Halloween Feast:** For foodies, hosting an annual Halloween dinner or potluck is a fun and delicious way to celebrate. Encourage your guests to bring dishes inspired by Halloween, such as "monster meatballs" or "witch's brew" punch. You can also incorporate

Halloween-themed table settings, like pumpkin centerpieces or black-and-orange color schemes.

1.4 Meaningful Traditions: Giving Back to the Community

Halloween doesn't just have to be about candy and costumes. It can also be a time to give back to the community and spread joy. Starting a tradition of community involvement can bring an extra layer of meaning to your Halloween celebrations.

- **Reverse Trick-or-Treating:** Instead of only collecting treats, why not give some back? Reverse trick-or-treating involves visiting neighbors or community centers and delivering small treats or goodies, especially to those who might not be able to participate in traditional trick-or-treating, such as elderly or homebound individuals.
- **Halloween Charity Drives:** Another way to give back is by organizing a Halloween charity drive. You can collect donations of candy, costumes, or other goods and deliver them to shelters, hospitals, or other organizations in need. This is a great way to spread the Halloween spirit while helping others in your community.

2. Embracing the Spirit of Halloween Year After Year

As Halloween evolves, it's important to embrace the spirit of the holiday in a way that resonates with you personally. Whether you love the spooky thrills, the creative costumes, or the time spent with loved ones, the key to keeping Halloween magical is staying true to what you enjoy most. Here are a few ways to ensure you keep the Halloween spirit alive year after year.

2.1 Cultivating a Sense of Wonder and Playfulness

At its heart, Halloween is a holiday that celebrates imagination, curiosity, and fun. To fully embrace its spirit, allow yourself to be playful and open to new experiences. Here's how:

- **Get Creative with Costumes:** Each year, challenge yourself to come up with a new costume that pushes your creativity. Whether it's a DIY project or an elaborate store-bought outfit, your costume is a chance to express yourself in a fun and imaginative way. Don't be afraid to think outside the box – you might surprise yourself with what you come up with!
- **Explore New Halloween Activities:** While it's important to honor traditions, trying something new each year can add excitement to the holiday. This could be visiting a new haunted house,

making a different kind of Halloween treat, or exploring a new neighborhood for trick-or-treating.

- **Stay Connected with the Community:** Halloween is a social holiday, so take advantage of the opportunity to connect with others. Attend local events like Halloween parades, festivals, or pumpkin patches, and don't be shy about striking up conversations with fellow Halloween enthusiasts.

2.2 Maintaining a Balance Between Tradition and Innovation

One of the joys of Halloween is balancing old traditions with fresh ideas. As the years go by, you may find that certain customs become beloved family rituals, while others fade away. It's okay to evolve your Halloween celebrations over time.

- **Keep What You Love:** Hold on to the traditions that bring you joy and make Halloween meaningful for you. This could be a specific pumpkin carving technique, a favorite movie you watch every October, or a particular event you attend every year. These are the elements that make Halloween feel special and personal.
- **Embrace Change:** As new trends and technologies emerge, don't hesitate to incorporate

them into your Halloween celebrations. Virtual Halloween parties, social media costume contests, and online haunted house tours are all modern twists on traditional activities. These innovations keep Halloween relevant and exciting for future generations.

2.3 Fostering a Sense of Community

Halloween isn't just about individual celebrations – it's also a time to bring people together. Whether it's your family, friends, or neighborhood, fostering a sense of community can enhance the magic of Halloween.

- **Neighborhood Events:** Organize or participate in neighborhood Halloween events, such as trick-or-treat block parties, pumpkin carving contests, or costume parades. These gatherings provide a chance for neighbors to connect and celebrate together, strengthening the community bond.
- **Involving Friends and Family:** Make Halloween a time to reconnect with loved ones. Whether it's by hosting an annual Halloween dinner or planning a group activity like visiting a corn maze or haunted house, involving friends and family in your celebrations can make the holiday even more memorable.

3. Celebrating Halloween Mindfully: Honoring the Past, Present, and Future

Halloween is a holiday rich in history, with roots that stretch back centuries. By honoring its origins while looking ahead to the future, we can celebrate Halloween in a way that feels meaningful and fulfilling. This final section will explore how to approach Halloween mindfully, incorporating elements of the past, present, and future into your traditions.

3.1 Reflecting on Halloween's Historical Significance

Halloween has its origins in the ancient Celtic festival of Samhain, a time when people believed the boundary between the living and the dead was blurred. While Halloween has transformed over time, many of its themes—such as honoring the dead and embracing the unknown—remain.

Take time each Halloween to reflect on the holiday's historical significance. You can do this by:

- **Exploring Halloween's History:** Learn about the different cultural traditions that have shaped Halloween, from Samhain to All Hallows' Eve to modern-day celebrations. Understanding the holiday's roots can deepen your appreciation for the customs you practice today.

- **Honoring the Dead:** In keeping with Halloween's ancient traditions, consider incorporating a moment of reflection to honor loved ones who have passed away. This could be as simple as lighting a candle in their memory or sharing stories about them during a Halloween gathering.

3.2 Savoring the Present Moment

While Halloween is often fast-paced, with parties, trick-or-treating, and haunted houses filling the schedule, it's important to savor the present moment. Mindful celebration means being fully present and enjoying each aspect of the holiday as it unfolds.

- **Slowing Down:** Take a moment to appreciate the sights, sounds, and smells of Halloween. Whether it's the crunch of fallen leaves, the glow of jack-o'-lanterns, or the taste of a warm apple cider, savor these sensory experiences and let them ground you in the present.
- **Enjoying Time with Loved Ones:** Halloween is a time for connection, so be sure to enjoy the company of your friends and family. Put away distractions like phones and fully immerse

yourself in the conversations, laughter, and joy that come with Halloween gatherings.

3.3 Looking Toward the Future

As Halloween continues to evolve, there are countless possibilities for how the holiday will be celebrated in the future. By remaining open to new ideas and traditions, you can ensure that Halloween remains a beloved part of your life for years to come.

- **Passing Down Traditions:** If you have children or younger family members, involve them in your Halloween traditions and share the stories behind them. This is a wonderful way to pass down the magic of Halloween to future generations.
- **Embracing Change:** As new generations add their own twist to Halloween, be open to incorporating these changes into your celebrations. Whether it's new technology, emerging trends, or evolving cultural customs, embracing change will keep Halloween vibrant and exciting for everyone.

Embracing the Magic of Halloween Year After Year

The magic of Halloween lies in its endless possibilities. It is a holiday that invites us to step outside the ordinary, celebrate our creativity, and connect with others. By creating your own traditions, embracing the playful spirit of the season, and honoring both the past and future of the holiday, you can ensure that Halloween remains a magical and meaningful part of your life year after year.

As you move forward, remember that there is no right or wrong way to celebrate Halloween. Whether you choose to stick to classic customs or invent entirely new ones, the most important thing is that your Halloween celebrations bring you joy, laughter, and a sense of wonder. So go ahead—carve those pumpkins, don your favorite costume, and let the magic of Halloween carry you through another unforgettable season.